TWELVE JEWS

TWELVE JEWS

Edited by
HECTOR BOLITHO

Essay Index Reprint Series

 BOOKS FOR LIBRARIES PRESS
FREEPORT, NEW YORK

First Published 1934
Reprinted 1967

INTERNATIONAL STANDARD BOOK NUMBER
0-8369-0223-8

LIBRARY OF CONGRESS CATALOG CARD NUMBER:
67-23179

PRINTED IN THE UNITED STATES OF AMERICA

CONTENTS

LIST OF ILLUSTRATIONS

INTRODUCTION

THIS book was planned long before the enforced exodus of the Jews from Germany, and it has no political significance, unless it shows how the Jew struggles towards honourable citizenship when the laws of the country allow him his self-respect, his freedom, and equal opportunity with his Christian contemporaries. Nor do I claim any fixed purpose behind this collection of twelve essays beyond a wish, which came to me some time ago, to exhibit the greatness of a number of Jews in a book free from propaganda ; for I have no axe to grind.

The quarrel between the Jews and the rest of civilisation has been kept alive by two forces : one, the peculiar character of the Jews, and the other, the antipathy of Christian or non-Jewish society. The one has induced the other. Centuries of estrangement from normal society and opportunity have undermined the qualities in Jewish character, so that Jews neither think nor act within the comprehension of other people. Christians therefore continue to withhold their sympathy from these sad, unhappy people. Even in enlightened modern States, where justice, tolerance, and freedom from superstition give some hope of human progress and some prospect of Jewish emancipation, the Jew remains a stranger. The mildest men, failing to understand the Jews, have become so irritated and alarmed by them that the intolerance of the Middle Ages will burn in them when the Jewish problem is spoken of. Many racial and moral inquisitions have faded from mankind ; but not this. It flourishes still, with only occasional glimpses of hope, but with many flashes of cruelty which make even the anti-Semitic wonder how much of the devil there is in man.

As an heir to the conventional Christian prejudice against the Jews, I travelled to Palestine two years ago, to try to understand the Zionist in what he hopefully calls his National home. After speaking to many Jews, and after seeing many of the Zionist settlements, in the beautiful valley of Jezreel, by the Jordan, and on the rich plain of Sharon, I returned to England in a turmoil of impressions and emotions. Although there was much that alarmed me in Palestine, there was enough in the sight of the Jews, radiant under the light of Zionism, to make me ashamed of my prejudices and anxious to believe in their cause.

From Palestine I went to Germany, where different Jews confronted me. Victimised and therefore shrewd and merciless, they did not seem to belong to the story of Herzl and Weizmann and the blossoming of Zion. In place of the young, blue-eyed Jewish farmer with whom I talked on the slopes where Jonathan was slain, I met the Jews who have incensed modern Germany. One was a cruel, dishonest business man in Berlin. When I talked to him of Palestine, he laughed, and he tried to deny his Jewish blood. He was nasty with Christian pretensions. The other was a cow-dealer on a farm in Oberhessen. One hundred years before, the cow-dealer's ancestors had been tortured in the little village. Yet they stayed. The cow-dealer himself had been stripped of his trousers by Nazi soldiers, who had painted their swastika upon his unwilling buttocks. The little man was warped—yet

he clung to the community which injured him, not
wholly embittered and not wholly despised. In the
next village, the Monds had lived in the seventeenth
and eighteenth centuries. They had been humble
and persecuted. But their courage had never been
destroyed. As my chapter on Ludwig Mond will show,
they rose valiantly above the circumstances of their
life, and one of them set forth, to cross the sea to
England, where riches and honour were given to
Christians and Jews in almost equal measure. I told
the little Jewish cow-dealer of this, and I asked him,
" Why don't you go away—to Palestine, where there
will be a certain kind of peace for you ? " He smiled.
No ; he would not go to a country full of Jews, where
there were no Christians to do business with.

I was dismayed. I remembered the zeal of the
farmer of Jezreel and, in the light of this, the apathy
of the German Jews perplexed me. I turned to a page
of Rathenau and I read :

> The Jews are no longer a nation, and they will never
> become one again. The endeavours of the Zionists are
> atavistic. The highly intellectual among the Jews have
> lost all national feeling, they recognise only individuals, in
> the same way as, in the future, there will be no nations—only
> individuals. It is the proletariat which holds the Jews
> together, which will not mix with the Aryan races, the others
> show no preference to a Jew above other people. The only
> thing which binds me to the Jews is, at the most, a feeling for
> ancestry, not even a feeling for family. That would be far
> too limited. An anti-French or anti-Russian person hurts
> me as much as an anti-Semitic. What life-purpose is there
> in this being " anti," i.e. " to hate " ? No ! we have no
> national feeling more. But the Germans must remain a
> nation and therefore our whole strength must be with them.

Two phrases in this passage helped me in my effort to understand my problem. Rathenau's blunt " The Jews are no longer a nation and they will never become one again." I felt this, all the time I was in Palestine, and I felt that it would not be in a National home nor in any trumpeting of causes that the Jews would find freedom from the mysterious bonds which hold them down. It will be through the growth of human nature among and in all nations that the Jew will be healed. For it is healing he needs, with no reckoning on the part of the giver as to gratitude, merit, response, or reward. Humanity can advance only as a whole : not at all while any race is handicapped or treated as pariahs. Only ideals and changes seen in relation to all mankind can benefit the world now. Even Fascism, with its cleansing forces, cannot erect higher barriers in a time when National barriers are being destroyed by human invention. How then can the Jews make a National home, unless it is that a home is a harbour and a place of healing ? The word National is fraught with perils.

Rathenau said also, " The highly intellectual among the Jews have lost all National feeling, they recognise only individuals." This statement astounded me, and I sat down with a piece of paper and made a list of great Jews to see how far Rathenau wrote the truth. The list was the beginning of this book. I thought it would be fascinating to pursue the story of each of the twelve Jews, and I added the names of the twelve writers whom I thought best capable of under-standing each of the subjects. With two exceptions, this first list is the one which appears on the Contents page of this book. The contributors have been allowed all freedom : the editorial guide given to them was no more than a sentence, outlining the nature of the book. So the contributors must be judged as twelve essayists, let loose to follow their own wishes and notions, not as twelve writers harnessed by an editor's idea and plan. My bag is mixed, and readers may be surprised to find Proust, who was only half a Jew, the late Lord Bearsted, and Mr. Jacob Epstein side by side.

At a time when Jewry is again upon the rack, these biographies may help calm people to realise the conquests as well as the sorrows of the race. Also, I hope, they will remind melancholy Jews of the courage and achievements of some of their own people.

HECTOR BOLITHO.

THE ATHENÆUM,
LONDON, S.W.
November, 1933.

THE FIRST LORD BEARSTED
BY HARTLEY WITHERS

THE FIRST LORD BEARSTED

THE FIRST LORD BEARSTED

By Hartley Withers

In the subject of this chapter we find the Jew playing the part in which he has done his best and most practical work for the world, and has earned the heartiest abuse—the part, that is, of financier and business organiser. Marcus Samuel made an immense fortune by cheapening the supply of oil and so making possible the development of the internal-combustion engine which has revolutionised transport by land and sea and has helped to create it by air. By his financial backing of Japan, at a crisis in her history, he assisted the rise of a power fraught with immense and perhaps formidable possibilities ; and during the Great War he worked for the cause of the Allies, in the matter of explosives, in a way that may have made all the difference to its result. In doing these things he was presenting an outstanding and exceptionally successful example of the work that his race has been doing all down the centuries for a world that has rewarded it with wealth, with such power as wealth brings with it, and with general unpopularity, except in some few countries that are really civilised.

This dislike of the Jewish financier and dealer is a nasty puddle that cannot be dodged in considering the work that the Jews have done and are doing. For it is, especially at the present moment when most of the world is in a specially bad and silly temper, an extremely important fact in the state of mind of the nations. The prominence of Jews in finance not only makes them unpopular, but also brings finance and the whole business of money-making and money-dealing into disfavour, with political effects that may have far-

reaching results. Whether Jews are unpopular because of their money, or money is unpopular because of
its Jews, is a question that might exercise the wits of a
suburban debating society ; but whichever be the hen
and whichever the egg, the fact remains that these two
unpopularities have reacted on and stimulated one another. This anti-Jewish prejudice, that makes some
muddle-headed people believe that there is something
unholy about the whole system of international finance,
originated, no doubt, in the Gospel story, and still,
perhaps, derives some of its virulence from that source.
At least, there is the well-known example of the English
sailor, who was discovered beating a Jew, and when
asked by his victim why, replied, " You crucified my
Gawd." " But all that happened two thousand years
ago " was a plea that had no weight. " Can't help
that," said the sailor, " I only heard about it last
night."

Seeing that Christians were, until comparatively
lately, quite ready to inflict hideous tortures on one
another on account of differences in points of doctrine,
the mediæval violence of the anti-Jew prejudice must
have been intense to a degree that can hardly be
imagined in these more tolerant days. And it was
increased by the money-making habits of the Jews,
which again were forced on them by the Christian
prejudice against usury, which made money-lending
to a great extent a Jewish monopoly. The race of
farmers, stock-keepers, and warriors depicted in the
books of the Old Testament was turned into a people
of money-dealers, pedlars, and middlemen, in the first
place because Christians were not allowed to lend
money at interest and so left this profitable field un-
tilled, and, in the second, because the Jews, being
subject at any moment to outbursts of persecution,
were obliged to keep their property in a form that

could easily be concealed or carried. For these purposes the precious metals and precious stones were evidently most convenient, and so the traffic in them tended to be concentrated in the hands of the people whom the Christians thus enriched by persecution. At the same time this necessity for concealing their wealth forced them to adopt habits which were regarded by their neighbours as miserly. Under the pressure of these influences there may well have emerged in the Middle Ages plenty of examples of the close-fisted Jew financier, such as we find depicted in Shylock, whose manners can hardly have been improved by the treatment that he received from his so-called Christian contemporaries. Antonio, the magnificent merchant and noble Venetian gentleman, when asking Shylock for a loan, admits that he is quite likely to spit on him and kick him, as he had done before.

In fact, the prejudice was so violent and so enduring, that even in the nineteenth century we find certain Christians perturbed by the Jewish birth of the Founder of their religion. At least, Heine observes that just as a Christian friend of his, a distinguished citizen of Hamburg, was seized with deep disgust whenever it occurred to him that his Saviour belonged to the unpleasant race which competed with him in spices and dyestuffs, so he, Heine, had a queasy feeling when he recognised that Shakespeare was an Englishman, and a member of " the most objectionable (*widerwärtig*) people that God has in His wrath created." [1]

All this had to be said, because I have to tell the story of a great financier and business organiser, and finance and big business are in these days under a very thick cloud, owing to mishaps and disasters for which they were by no means wholly responsible.

[1] Shakespeare's *Mädchen und Frauen*.

Also, the subject of my story stands here as a Jew. So before I can begin it, it was necessary to show why it was that the Jews became especially skilled in finance, and how it was that their skill in finance, itself an unattractive quality to the great majority of spend-thrift humanity, was mixed up with other causes of prejudice against them and so has produced an un-savoury mixture of muddle-headed suspicion which makes it difficult for many quite sensible people to see anything interesting or good in the career of a successful financier. " The word banker," as one of them lately observed, " is now synonymous with bandit." People have somehow got it into their heads that the machinery of finance sucks the lifeblood out of industry and flourishes while all the rest of the world is languishing in depression. In fact finance can only prosper when it has prosperous industry behind it. It earns its living by financing the produc-tion and distribution of the goods that industry makes and handles, and by fertilising the world with top-dressings of capital and credit, which—apart from occasional and short-lived swindles—only bring profit to the financiers who do the work when the final result is an increase of real wealth.

In this work of financing international trade and production, the peculiar position of the Jews has en-abled them to play a specially useful part. Scattered all over the world, with relations and connections in many countries, they have always had a unique know-ledge of the languages and business usages and money systems of the different nations. Their separate race and religion have kept them free from the prejudices of extreme nationalism which have so often blinded the Gentile citizens of the countries in which they dwelt. In a world which is only just beginning to see that economic interdependence is inevitable, and that full prosperity can come to no country unless it is shared with others, the Jews have long recognised that national barriers are an impediment to business, and that if mankind wants to enter into the full possession of the wealth that science and invention have made possible, it can only do so by co-operating in its production and distribution, instead of quarrelling about its division. Any dealer in exchange—that mysterious traffic which enables the money of one country to be turned into that of another with a celerity and dispatch that is hardly rivalled by any other kind of business— must have mind and eyes always wide open to all the influences that may affect the values of the currencies of all the nations that have any importance in the markets of the world. Any event, political or economic, that affects the earning power of a country will react on the value of its money in the exchange market. Dealers in exchange thus have to have an exceptionally finely developed international sense ; and if they are to prosper must have exceptional facilities for following the course of events abroad and exceptional sagacity in interpreting their economic significance. And the Jews have been, all down the ages, active dealers in exchange and traffickers in bills drawn abroad and drawn on distant countries. The work that they have done, by thus assisting to bind the whole world into one great market, not only trained them in breadth of mind, but also had an immense influence in promoting the growth of international trade and raising the general standard of comfort, until this miserable and discreditable crisis, out of which we are just beginning to struggle, put back the economic clock. The chief cause of it was an attempt on the part of various nations, under the influence of different kinds of panic and hysteria—mostly political in origin—to undo the work of international finance and shut themselves up in watertight compartments. In such circumstances international finance had no choice but to close down its activities and put up its shutters and wait for mankind to return to a saner frame of mind. And then mankind accuses it of having caused the crisis.

In these days, thanks to the better distribution of wealth, which is one of the good things that the Great War left behind it, the activity of Jews in business has been most notably shown by the provision of cheap articles for the million. The Montagu Burtons, Markses (of Marks and Spencer), Salmon and Glucksteins, Lyonses and many others have shown the world both how to distribute and to produce, at prices within the reach of a public that was enormously expanded by cheapness and organisation, articles and services that were formerly reserved for the enjoyment of a minority. In other words, they have been helping to solve the problem—so discreditable to our intelligence, that it should be a problem at all—of getting into consumption some of the greatly increased wealth that business is eager to provide, if it could feel assured of a market. In the Middle Ages, their most important clients were naturally the monarchs. William the Conqueror, with his keen practical eye for useful helpers, invited them to England, and there can be no doubt that their services as the " royal usurers " enabled him and his successors to carry out the immensely important work of founding a strong central government, in marked contrast with the feudal sectionalism that was destined for many centuries to disturb the peace of Europe and retard its economic progress.

Under the Norman kings the Jews were favoured and petted. In fact, a story is told by Hume, in his *History of England*, which shows that William Rufus

not only found them useful as money-lenders, but had
no prejudice against their religious doctrines.

> As an instance of his irreligion, [says the historian] we
> are told that he once accepted of sixty marks from a Jew
> whose son had been converted to Christianity and who
> engaged him by that present to assist him in bringing back
> the youth to Judaism. William employed both menaces
> and persuasion for that purpose, but finding the convert
> obstinate in his new faith, he sent for the father—

and paid him back half the money.

In Lord Bearsted we find one who worked both for
Governments and for a world-wide public, having
earned the power to do so by sheer force of his energy,
enterprise, and determination. Those who think
that no business career is really " romantic " unless
it begins in the gutter, have tried to confer upon him
an extra distinction by supposing him to have arisen
from a more than humble origin. In fact, he was
born in Whitechapel in 1853, second son of a father
who had already earned an assured and respected position among the Jews of that always strongly Jewish
neighbourhood, and had laid the foundations of the
business in which young Marcus Samuel was destined
to train himself for wider enterprises. This business
consisted in manufacturing and trading in fancy articles,
among which were the shell-covered boxes, inscribed
" A Present from Margate," or any other seaside place
of popular resort, that were carried back to the suburban homes of Victorian trippers ; and the name
" Shell," still so prominent in the advertisement pages
of the newspapers, and at the petrol-filling stations on
arterial roads and in country lanes, had its origin in the
affection felt by the founder of the world-wide oil
enterprise for this detail of the business in which his
youthful experiences had been gained. Although,

however, Lord Bearsted's origin by no means dated
from extreme poverty, it was certainly far removed
from opulence ; and he was fond of relating, in the
days when he had acquired immense wealth and a
Peerage, how, when he started his municipal career as
alderman of an East-End ward, he was nearly rejected
by the Aldermanic body as being too poor and undistinguished to take his place in its highly respectable
ranks.

All the products of all countries and climates find a
mart in Whitechapel, but the family business of the
Samuels seems to have been chiefly concerned with
Eastern articles ; and after an education begun in
Edmonton and continued in Brussels, where he acquired a useful mastery of conversational French,
business with the East absorbed most of Marcus
Samuel's attention, as he began to look for openings
for his ambitions and activities. One of the early
enterprises that marked him as a man with an exceptionally wide eye for a trade opening was an opera-
tion by which he poured an opportune supply of rice
into India, then afflicted by one of the famines that
were formerly a frequent feature in her history.

But it was, of course, through his work for the production and distribution of petroleum that he won the
wealth and power that enabled him to render such
signal service to the cause of the Allies, and to crown
his career by being described by Lord Birkenhead, in
his *Contemporary Personalities*, as " one of the great
men of our day."

Anyone who has undressed in his youth, on a dark
winter's night, by the dim obscurity of a rushlight, can
testify to the immense difference that was made, for
the majority of the inhabitants of the world, by the
cheapening of the production of oil as an illuminant.
This event happened, owing to the ingenuity of

American engineers, a few years after Marcus Samuel was born, and the business of supplying this new source of light among the customers with whom he had established connections in the East, was an enterprise that appealed to his imagination, by reason of its unbounded possibilities. In its early days oil production was an even more speculative proposition than gold mining. A well-known figure in the pages of American comic writers is a plausible gentleman selling shares in oil companies with incalculable possibilities, and the fortunes made and lost by gambling in " lots " alleged to be oleiferous have provided many a text for moralists. A commodity that is found underground, in problematical quantity that may be seriously diminished by boring operations undertaken by a rival in the near neighbourhood, is evidently, in the early days of its exploitation, most likely to attract the attention of those who prefer the brilliance of speculation to the solidity of investment ; and even those who confined their energies to its handling and distribution must have known that in the matter of procuring supplies, they would be faced with formidable difficulties from the nature, both of the product and, in some cases at least, of the producers.

Such was the enterprise into which Marcus Samuel threw his youthful imagination and activities, casting an ever-widening net in his search both for sources of supply and for outlets of distribution. Sooner than most, he saw that the day of the big battalions was at hand both in industry and commerce. His rivals and opponents he fought with a spirit that sometimes induced them to join forces rather than meet his competition ; but at the same time he made friendly connections with a number of firms engaged in the Eastern trade, introducing, in his field of operations, that principle of cooperation and combination which has since then made such gigantic strides and has incidentally undermined the conclusions of certain chapters in economic text-books, which made competition the corner-stone of the science.

Along these lines he worked with such success that the Shell Transport and Trading Company, perpetu-ating and carrying all over the world the memory of the Margate shell-boxes, was formed in 1897 with a capital of £1,800,000 in shares of £100. No public issue was made and the capital was all placed among those con-nected with the various enterprises and their friends and connections ; and it was not until 1902 that the general public was invited to partake in the enterprise through an issue of preference shares. The prospectus inviting subscriptions stated that the company had been formed " for the purpose of amalgamating the interests, combining under one management and con-tinuing the development of the transport of illumi-nating oil mainly by means of tank steamers and its storage in bulk, sale and distribution in India, China, Japan, and the Straits created by," a long list of firms, including M. Samuel & Co. and Samuel, Samuel & Co., whose preponderating influence in the group was shown by the adoption of the name chosen. At its inception, this enterprise was thus chiefly a distributing business, and it is interesting to note that in the first years of its existence such of its shares as were quoted in the official list of the Stock Exchange were included among shipping securities. Nevertheless, even when the first prospectus was issued, it was already turning its atten-tion to the production of the commodity that it carried, stored, and distributed ; for we find a reference to large oil-producing territories taken over by the company in Dutch Borneo.

This early invasion of Dutch Borneo in search of supplies, nearer to the Eastern market than the oil of

Baku, may have marked the beginning of a struggle which ended, in 1907, in amalgamation with the Royal Dutch Petroleum Company. To carry this into effect, as the *Oil and Petroleum Year Book* tells us, two new companies were formed, the Anglo-Saxon Petroleum Co., Ltd., registered in England with a capital of £25,000,000, and the Bataafsche Petroleum Maatschappij, registered in Holland with a capital of 300,000,000 florins (then equivalent to about the same figure). The Shell Company holds 40 per cent of the capital of both companies and the Royal Dutch Company 60 per cent. Moreover, the Royal Dutch Company acquired, as from January 1, 1907, 500,000 ordinary shares at 30s. each from shareholders in the Shell. (The original £100 shares had by this time been converted, or multiplied, into shares of £1.)

Since then the capital of the Shell Company has been increased to £43,000,000, and any detailed account of its ramifications and connections would take us too far away from the story of its founder. But one or two more figures, illustrative of the practical work of the gigantic combination that he organised, may be included here. According to the authority quoted above, the total production of crude oil of the Royal Dutch-Shell group, and of the companies in which it was interested was, in 1931 (a year of intense depression), 20,532,758 metric tons, of which Venezuela contributed over 7½ millions, the United States of America nearly 5 millions, and the Dutch East Indies nearly 4 millions. It may also be noted that the number of companies with Shell in their titles, included in the *Year Book's* survey, is forty-two.

As we saw, oil for purposes of illumination was the subject of the early activities of Marcus Samuel. For this purpose, the utility of oil has in these days retired into the background, owing to the much greater importance of its use as motive-power and lubricant, and for other purposes, in which it touches the lives of all of us so closely that it is accepted as one of those things without which modern civilisation could not exist. But it never could have achieved its position as a necessary of modern life if the problem of its transport had not been solved by the founders of the Shell Transport Company. Getting a thing from the place where it is made, grown, or found, to the places where it is wanted is one of the most important links in the chain that gives it value ; because, until it has reached the place where it is wanted, it is still a commodity looking for a buyer ; and its value depends on what somebody will give for it who is prepared to face the risk and cost of conveying it to its final market. This elementary economic fact is well illustrated by the hoary anecdote of the Scottish drover and the English meat merchant. The drover was selling beasts at a fair in the Highlands, and the Smithfield salesman, watching the proceedings as a relief to the boredom of a holiday, told the Scotsman that the prices he was getting were absurd, and that if he took his cattle to London, they would put much bigger sums into his pocket. " Vera true," said the drover, " and if I could take Loch Lomond to Hell, I could sell it at half a croon a glass."

Oil was a particularly difficult commodity to transport by sea, because of its unsavoury effects on the hulls of ships, and their consequent unsuitability for other kinds of cargo on a return voyage. Until this disadvantage could be overcome, oil was what shippers call a one-way freight, and had to be sold at a price that would cover two voyages, out and homeward. Samuel adopted a system of cleaning out the hull with steam, said to have been suggested to him by the master of a trading vessel, and to him and his group must also be ascribed the momentous discovery of the possibilities of oil as liquid fuel. It will be remembered that in the first prospectus issued by the Shell Company reference was made to an oil-producing property in Borneo, and it was from the handling of Borneo oil that this use was hit on and made practical. Marcus Samuel told the story himself in an article contributed to the *London and China Express*, and quoted in a book entitled *The Shell that Hit Germany Hardest*, published by the Shell Marketing Company. He relates that petroleum struck in Kotei, East Borneo,

> proved of very heavy specific gravity and threatened great difficulties in finding a market. So we decided to adapt our ships to burning it as fuel under their boilers. This was so successful that we urged it upon the British Government, giving them every opportunity of seeing it working, and for their better conviction bringing home a steamer under liquid fuel from Borneo *via* the Cape to London. The steamer (the *Murex*), which accomplished this historic voyage, brought petrol in bulk the first time it has ever been so carried, constituting another record for British enterprise.

Besides carrying out this pioneer work with liquid fuel, the Shell Companies have girdled the earth with a belt of supply stations, so that it is possible for a fleet to make a voyage round the world on fuel drawn entirely from Shell sources of production.

> Thus, [according to the officially published saga] in Suez there are the supplies from the Egyptian fields ; in India there are Karachi, Bombay, Calcutta, Madras, and Colombo (Ceylon), and in the Straits Settlements, Singapore. The Pacific is supplied by the Shell Company of California. In the Far East are the Dutch Indies and Sarawak, the main sources of Shell supply ; and in Mexico, Trinidad, and Venezuela there are further Shell associations. Large installations for the storage of fuel liquid are maintained at

both ends of the Panama Canal, also in China and Australia : and additions are constantly being made to the various depots throughout the world.

And further :

The peculiar character of the Borneo oil, which proved so vital a factor in winning the War, has led to the discovery of extremely valuable by-products. No less than 12,000 tons of paraffin wax per year, many millions sterling in value, are extracted. Varnish is also manufactured, and last but by no means least, the oil is the source of a great series of base dye products which threaten the pre-War German monopoly in this important market.

This passage brings us to the first Lord Bearsted's chief claim to have served his country with specially effective distinction. In 1898 he had been knighted for services rendered in connection with the salvaging of H.M.S. *Victorious*. In 1903 he was made a baronet to show that he had worthily upheld the dignity of the office of Lord Mayor of London. In 1915 the Shell shareholders learnt that their chairman had received a letter from the Lords of the Admiralty expressing their appreciation of the war services rendered by their company. The story of these services was fully told in an article in the *Petroleum Review*, published shortly after the War, which stated that

it was in consequence of special petroleum products being able to fill such a vital rôle with success that the Allied victory was assured.

For this statement the authority was quoted of M. Bérenger, the Commissioner-General of Petroleum in France, who, referring at a banquet to the invaluable assistance rendered by the Shell group in connection with the supply of toluol to the Allied Governments for high explosives, had said that without these supplies, the War could not possibly have been won by the Allies.

Borneo oil, mentioned already in connection with the discovery of the use of liquid fuel, is again in the picture on this grimmer occasion. For it appears that though it had long been known that toluol exists in various petroleums, none was known from which so high a percentage of toluol could be extracted as that which could be obtained from the Borneo oils. This discovery had been made through investigations carried out at Cambridge some time before the War, and the product of these examinations was offered to the British Government by the Shell group, and was not at first accepted. When, however, an offer to the French Government had been made and accepted, the British Government was again approached before the final closing of the agreement ; and in the meantime Lord Moulton and his Explosives department had been searching in vain for supplies of toluol, and the output of high explosives had been suffering. Accepted at long last, the Shell's offer, under which more than half the supply of toluol went to Britain and the rest to the Allies, made possible that increase in the output of high explosives without which the War could not have been won.

Marcus Samuel's part in carrying through these arrangements can be traced in the sketch of these events given in Lord Birkenhead's portrait of him in *Contemporary Personalities.*

> When, [he wrote] we entered on that great struggle we were almost in extremity. Our affairs were seriously disturbed within ; it was difficult for innovators to get a hearing. It seems providential now that persistence gained the day. It is lucky that Mr. Winston Churchill was in charge of the Admiralty on the outbreak of hostilities, and that for some twenty years from the year 1892 the name of Admiral

Fisher had guaranteed efficiency and far-sightedness in the
Navy. It was, in fact, Lord Fisher who became Chairman
of the Royal Commission on Oil Fuel in 1912. Meanwhile
Sir Marcus Samuel, as another admiral, long after the War
was over, declared, never left the authorities alone until all
his points were practically conceded. The support of Lord
Fisher was a great gain. But in season and out of season the
pioneer himself had to be continually hammering at the
Admiralty doors. Yet that was not enough. There came
a time when our material resources were quite inadequate
to carry out plans for making high explosives in England.
A refinery was imported from Holland, England as a whole
little dreaming that such an undertaking had even been contemplated. The German menace was at its height. Many
another experiment had to be carried out with similar contempt for the risks that must be run. But these things were
accomplished in such a way that Lord Bearsted is entitled
to be regarded as one of the deliverers of his country.

Concerning the shipping of that refinery from
Holland, surely one of the most extraordinary of our
war-time achievements, a little more detail may be
taken from the Shell's own narrative. It relates that
in the spring of 1915, when the Company's offer to
supply toluol was adopted, no distillery for extracting
it was available in England, and so it was decided to
transfer, lock, stock and barrel, a suitable plant possessed by it in Rotterdam.

Speed was vital. Men were being killed every day in
France whose lives would have been preserved by an adequate supply of high-explosive ammunition. To save a
day was to save precious lives. In an incredibly short
space of time, the distillery was dismantled and shipped on
a steamer specially chartered for the purpose by the Government, which, contrary to all regulations, left Rotterdam
after dark. Had a lucky torpedo from a U-boat found its
mark in her, the course of the entire War might have been
altered . . . When the vessel appeared at dawn off the

English coast she was met and escorted into the Port of London by British destroyers. Special orders had been issued officially to the London dock authorities to have the vessel unloaded with the greatest possible dispatch. Lighters and tugs were already in attendance, and swung the cargo up on a flowing tide to Brentford, where railway trucks lay waiting to convey the precious equipment across England. Some sections of the weird plant were as large as 10 feet in diameter. The railway line from Brentford to Portishead was cleared to safeguard against hitch or delay. In the morning the trucks were at Portishead. Here, again, speed and organisation had seized time by the forelock. Land had been acquired, foundations laid, and walls raised. Cranes stood at attention waiting to swing the apparatus into place . . . As a result of this exceptional piece of organisation and co-operation between the Government and Shell, the distillery which it would in the ordinary course of things have taken many months to build and equip, was in full swing in the extraordinarily short period of six weeks.

This feat, implemented by the rapid erection of further plants in other parts of England for the conversion of toluol into T.N.T., by no means completed the tale of the war services rendered by the organisation founded and developed by Marcus Samuel. In 1917 there came a tank tonnage crisis owing to the losses of oil-carrying tanks through submarine attacks, and the immense demands for liquid fuel for the Navy. Oil tankers were hunted with special zest by the U-boats, whose commanders knew well that nearly the whole of the British fleet, with its auxiliary cruisers, was depending entirely on liquid fuel. Since the Shell group had discovered the application of liquid fuel to purposes of marine transport, it was obviously its business to deal with the crisis produced by scarcity of oil carriers. Which it duly did, by proposing to the Admiralty that liquid fuel might be imported in

the double-bottoms or ballast tanks of ordinary merchant ships, which system it had itself successfully
adopted many years before. The work of conversion
could be carried out in shipyards overseas, and so
would entail no claims on the labour force of the
overworked yards at home ; and as to the time involved, another obvious objection, the Shell people
promptly dealt with that by converting a cargo boat,
sent to Hong Kong for the purpose, in two months
and two days. By this method, " during the most
critical period, as much as 125,000 tons of oil was
carried in one month, and by the date of the signing of
the armistice, 1,014,570 tons of liquid fuel had been
safely brought over."

Besides these outstanding achievements, many pages
might be filled with the war-time records of the Shell
companies in organising the supply of motive-power
behind the lines, and for tanks and aeroplanes. They
can boast that from the very beginning of the War right
up to the summer of 1917 every gallon of aviation spirit
supplied to the Allied Flying Corps was Shell. By
that time the Air Force had grown to such a size that
it was no longer possible to keep pace with the demand,
though the entire output of " Shell aviation " was
absorbed by it up to the end of the War. Certainly
the title of the " Shell that hit Germany hardest " can
fairly be claimed by the organisation of which Lord
Bearsted was the potent driving-wheel, and, as has been
shown, the effective and persistent representative, who
kept hammering at the doors of the powers that be.

In the light of recent events in Germany it is interesting to note that while Marcus Samuel was working
with such determination and success for the cause of
England and the Allies, another Jew was organising
supplies of essential materials for Germany, without
which it would have been impossible for her soldiers

to win the admiration of the world by their magnificent military effort. In his *Walther Rathenau, Sein Leben und Sein Werk*, Harry Graf Kessler relates how the organisation of supply of materials (*Rohstoffs Organisation*) created by Rathenau had saved wide areas of the German Empire from the fate that befell the northern district of France,

> for without them the German army could only have defended the frontiers during a few months.

This writer states that staff officers at the front believed in October 1914 that it would not be possible for Germany to continue the war beyond the following spring, owing to scarcity of nitrate and saltpetre. "Die Katastrophe ist nur durch die Tätigkeit von Walther Rathenau abgewendet worden."

It need hardly be said that his successful work as pioneer in a new, profitable industry, extraordinarily rapid in its growth, brought immense wealth, at a pace as fast as the progress of his enterprises, to Marcus Samuel. In 1895, when still in his early forties, he bought the estate known as the Mote, near Maidstone, with its deer-park of 600 acres and all the contents of its mansion. When the War came he turned his country house into a hospital, but continued to live there and to make sure, by his active presence, that its wounded inmates received every possible attention that could secure their comfort and assist their recovery. Mention has already been made of the titles and civic honours that rewarded his public services. In 1925 they were rounded off by a Peerage, when he entered the House of Lords as Viscount Bearsted of Maidstone. He was also Commander of the Order of Leopold of Belgium ; and his timely services in backing the first Japanese loan issued in London, and his long business connections with the Far East, made him a

Knight Commander of the Rising Sun. Cambridge, Sheffield, and other Universities approved his zeal and generosity in the cause of scientific research with honorary degrees. In the City, the acceptances of the private banking firm founded by him and his family were rated with the best of the " gilt-edged " bills.

During his term of office as Lord Mayor he attended, in civic state, a service at the New Synagogue, then in Great St. Helen's. He also showed what he thought of countries which treated members of his race in a manner of which he did not approve, by refusing to entertain the Rumanian Minister at the Lord Mayor's banquet. At the same time he was no narrow bigot, and his benefactions to hospitals and to the cause of education were distributed without any prejudices dictated by religion or race. He was, as recorded by *The Times* in its obituary notice, the first to respond to the appeal, published by it on July 3, 1922, for help to preserve the fabric of St. Paul's. His cheque for £1,000 was sent by his wife with a note saying, " My husband, who is unfortunately very ill, desires me to state that, as an ex-Lord Mayor of the City of London who has so frequently joined in worship at St. Paul's Cathedral on great State occasions, he is anxious to join in maintaining the Civic Cathedral."

From the same authority we learn that after the Curragh incident in March 1914, he telegraphed to *The Times* from Biarritz an offer of £10,000 to start a fund for the relief of the families of officers " who have resigned their commissions and risked the ruin of their careers rather than spill the blood of loyal subjects of His Majesty."

He married, in 1881, Fanny Elizabeth, only daughter of Benjamin Benjamin, who died a few hours before him in January 1927. They had two sons, of whom the younger was killed in the War, and two daughters.

Fishing and literature were his recreations, and both he and his wife were keenly interested, as expert collectors, in the creations of Oriental arts and crafts.

Such was Marcus Samuel, and such was the work that he did for himself and his race and his country and the world in general. He was a typical example of the millionaire financier and organiser. Do we need this type of man to forward enterprise and make and develop new discoveries ? Or is he, as many will tell us, an economic excrescence whose huge gains and power are a symptom of the weakness of the capitalist system ?

It is evident that as long as the vast majority of people prefer an easy-going life, and do not want to be bothered by striking out new lines of thought and action, the man who will take big risks and wear out his energies by looking for new openings in production and trade must be encouraged to do so by some kind of reward ; and further, that it will pay the rest of us handsomely to give it to him, or rather, to let him collect it out of our pockets, as long as that reward takes the form of money. Most of us members of the common herd are constitutionally lazy and timid. We do our work, such as it is, as well as we can, for our own satisfaction and because we want to keep the wolf from the door, but we do not look for new openings or take new responsibilities if we can avoid it. Fortunately for us there is a small minority of people who are built otherwise. They are born with a craving to get things done, to push things along, and to look for new lines of wealth-getting. Along with this restless eagerness, they are often born with an uncanny flair for business openings and for the kind of article that the general public is going to want, or can be persuaded to want. These qualities, sometimes combined with a certain ruthlessness of method, make the man who organises enterprise and creates Big Business. He supplies the driving power which applies the discoveries of the inventor and the scientist, who are generally quite unpractical people, to the furtherance of our comfort and happiness. Whatsoever be the economic system under which mankind works for its living, the services of the organiser will always be wanted, and until we are all born organisers, his services will command some sort of premium.

As to the huge rewards that such human driving wheels acquire and the gigantic power that it is supposed to give them, it is easy to exaggerate both. Some gain millions, but against this we must set the financial bones of the many pioneers which lie scattered along the road of human progress because their owners lacked the right flair or the necessary luck. Perhaps the day will come when the successful pioneers will be sufficiently rewarded with a title and a gold chain, and to those fastidious folk who regard all accumulations of money as a sordid vulgarity, this will be an improvement on the present arrangement. In the meantime, the millions that they get do not do the rest of us much harm. All that they can do with them is to hand them back to the rest of us, by either spending them (often on things that are a nuisance and a bore to their generally simple-minded possessors) or investing them in fresh enterprise, or giving them away. The power that is conferred on them by their money is very strictly limited by public opinion. For the Big Business man is highly sensitive, especially in these critical days, to the breath of public disfavour ; and when he spends and gives, the object must be one that the rest of the community, or a sufficiently influential section of it, will approve. When he invests, he is equally, or perhaps even more, tied in his choice of enterprise. For unless he earns a profit, he will not only lose his money, but his fame as an organiser of financial victory will be smirched. And profit can only be earned if he supplies the public with something that it wants at a price that it can pay. In other words, he has to tax his energies in devising schemes to promote the comfort of you and me.

BENJAMIN DISRAELI
EARL OF BEACONSFIELD

By John Hayward

BENJAMIN DISRAELI, EARL OF BEACONSFIELD

BENJAMIN DISRAELI
EARL OF BEACONSFIELD

By John Hayward

" Der alte Jude, das ist der Mann."—Bismarck on Disraeli, 1878.

" Nature has given me an awful ambition and fiery passions." Such magniloquence on the lips of a " damned bumptious Jew boy " must have seemed strangely conceited to the vast, insensible mass of the English middle class, which had just witnessed the passing of the great Reform Bill of 1832. It was certainly an unpropitious moment for romantic gestures or movements. Lord Byron would have understood what Benjamin d'Israeli meant by these words ; but Lord Byron, though still very much alive on the Continent, was dead as far as England was concerned. Beckford, who had so much in common with this young Jew and whose wild enormity of Gothic magnanimity at Fonthill would certainly have delighted him, did understand this much : " What appeared conceit in d'Israeli," he confided to a friend, " was only the irrepressible consciousness of superior power." But Beckford, then, was an outcast from society, whose opinion could do far more harm than good to an ambitious young man. The future, however, was to confirm this judgment, and was to justify the confidence which from the very beginning Disraeli himself had in his own powers : " The World calls me conceited," he said. " The World is in error. . . . When I was considered very conceited indeed I was nervous and had self-confidence only by fits. . . . I am only truly great in action. If ever I am placed in a truly eminent position, I shall prove this. I could rule the House of Commons, although there would be

43

great prejudice against me at first." He did, in fact, prove it triumphantly; and he did indeed rule the House of Commons, though there was, as he had anticipated, intense prejudice against him at first, which some of his enemies never entirely overcame.

The World nevertheless was not altogether without a cause for its misgiving. In this country suspicion is easily roused by any appearance of the odd or unconventional either in looks or behaviour. The World looked and drew its conclusions from what it saw.

> He came up Regent Street [we are told] when it was crowded, in his blue surtout, a pair of military light blue trousers, black stockings with red stripes, and shoes.

And as the World divided to allow this strange portent to pass

> it was [records an eyewitness] like the opening of the Red Sea, which I now perfectly believe from experience.

But it was not alone the habit that marked him out in an age when clothes were brighter and more variegated than they are now, but the almost Oriental complexion—smooth, sallow, even a little unhealthy; the gloved and ornately be-ringed fingers; and most conspicuously the oleaginous raven curls artfully disposed about the nape of the neck. In this startling get-up, and armed with the arrogance and uneasy assurance of one who is acutely sensitive to public opinion, though fighting all the while against a sense of inferiority and misprision, common to one of his race, Disraeli—as he decided to spell his name—strove for a place in London Society. Fifty years later, old, infirm, and within twelve months of his death, when not only London but the great homes of England had accepted him, he was compelled even so to deny in public that he had ever

actually worn in his youth the green velvet trousers in
which popular legend had clothed him.

If he entered the struggle exquisitely arrayed, he
also entered it carefully and indeed remarkably prepared in other respects. Voice, gestures, mannerisms
alike were as sedulously polished as his boots. In the
brilliant series of letters to his sister, written in his early
twenties, while he was indulging on the Continent a
precocious taste for luxury and the sublimely elegant
in food, wine, music, women, architecture, and scenery,
we can trace the rapid development of those gifts which
before very long were to bring him fame as a novelist
and invitations to the most exclusive drawing-rooms
of Mayfair and Belgravia. Yet these gifts—satire,
sarcasm so biting that it was mistaken at times for
rudeness, epigram, wit in its old metaphysical sense,
a vocabulary rich in unusual words and seductive
images, and, not least, an extraordinary turn for placing
his remarks in conversation to their best advantage—
were all part of an elaborate defence against ridicule.
His hypersensitive nature could not face the world
unprotected ; but this protective armour, even when
youthful timidity and self-consciousness had been successfully mastered, never wholly concealed the ardour
of a profoundly romantic temperament. Later, it is
true, the cares of office and the grinding anxieties inseparable from political life dimmed much of his early
precocity, and he chose in the end to mask his feelings
in silence rather than in words. The inner fire,
however, never burnt itself out. After nearly half a
century in the House of Commons, it suddenly leapt
into flame in the pages of *Lothair* :

> The sun had set in glory over the broad expanse of waters
> still glowing in the dying beam ; the people were assembled
> in thousands on the borders of the lake, in the centre of

which was an island with a pavilion. Fanciful barges and
gondolas of various shapes and colours were waiting for
Lothair and his party, to carry them over to the pavilion,
where they found a repast which became the hour and the
scene : coffee and ices and whimsical drinks, which sultanas
would sip in Arabian tales. No sooner were they seated
than the sound of music was heard, distant, but now nearer,
till there came floating on the lake, until it rested before the
pavilion, a gigantic shell, larger than the building itself, but
holding in its golden and opal seats Signor Mardoni and all
his orchestra.

" My books," he was never tired of saying, " are
the history of my life."   In them, as well as in his
letters, the conflict between the dreamer and the man
of action is more pronounced than in his life.   " I am
never well save in action," he repeated to his friend
Lady Blessington, " and then I feel immortal."   Without the lust for power and an inexhaustible capacity for
the labour necessary to attain it, he might well have
slipped back into the world of dreams and romantic
speculation conjured up by a singularly fertile imagination.   That world indeed was never far away.   Even
in his sixtieth year, we find him writing to that benevo-
lent old Jewess Mrs. Brydges Williams : " It is a
privilege to live in this age of rapid and brilliant events.
What an error to consider it a utilitarian age.   It is one
of infinite romance ! "   And, to another correspondent,
ten years later : " I sigh for moonlight.   I think I
could live and love in that light for ever."

Thus, in fiction at least, he gave expression to
dreams and desires that were never adequately fulfilled for him in life, and largely on this account his
novels were immensely successful in what was after
all for many people the drab, utilitarian world of
Bright and Cobden.   One of them—*Coningsby*—was
both the inspiration and, as it were, the manifesto of

that eager and exalted parliamentary group known as
" Young England."

But it was not only that in them he satisfied a
passionate predilection for the embellishments of culture, and recaptured some of the glamour of the
exotic which had been revealed to him as a youth
in his wanderings across Europe and as far as the
Holy Sepulchre ; he declared also his belief—and it
is essentially Jewish—in the value of the prerogatives
of the monarch and the privileges of the aristocracy,
the influence of traditions and institutions and the
sanctity of property. Furthermore, he professed,
though not so emphatically as in his one ambitious
poem, *The Revolutionary Epic*, a confidence in democracy, which was to surprise his political friends and
confirm the accusation of opportunism repeatedly
brought against him by his enemies. He believed
then in what many have tried and failed to believe
since—the fundamental conservatism of the working
classes. In *Sybil* he recorded, and was never to forget, the bleakness and squalid affluence of the places
he had visited on a tour through the industrial North.
Age, it is true, softened his memories of the poverty
and injustice he had witnessed, but enough remained
to keep him from the narrowest conservatism and to
compel him afterwards to introduce legislation for the
reform of the factory system. Incidentally his sympathy with the proletariat led many men to suppose
that he was at heart a Liberal and that his allegiance to
the Tory Party was simply a matter of expediency,
due to his having seized the opportunity, at the repeal
of the Corn Laws, to turn Peel out of office.

His veneration for institutions is evident in his attitude to religion, though here again he was to be accused
of time-serving. " There are few great things left,"
he wrote, " and the Church is one." Disraeli had been

baptized in the Christian faith, and throughout his life was a regular communicant. In this he saw himself carrying out part of the individual's duty to the State —the maintenance and promotion of the established Church. Nor did he regard this as inconsistent with his pride in Jewry, nor in what he believed was its inalienable heritage. " Race," he insisted, " is the key to history " ; and it was his unalterable conviction that his race were the elect of God. For, as he attempts to show, with much feeling but little authority, in a celebrated parenthesis in his biography of Lord George Bentinck, and more fully, though not more eloquently, in *Tancred*, the Jews are " by an inexorable law of Nature " a superior people ; in them alone did God confide on the slopes of Mount Sinai ; and for them, at any rate in the first place, Christ died. This, briefly, was " the great Arian mystery " over which his romantic feeling for the past perpetually hovered.

A member of a race, deep-rooted in an indeterminable antiquity, vestiges of which, as he had seen for himself, were still preserved in the customs and institutions of the natives of Palestine and Arabia, Disraeli was thus instinctively and naturally conservative in his attitude to society. The conduct of his life, both at home and in politics, though with notable inconsistencies in the latter, which, as we have hinted, led to widespread mistrust of his motives and at times even of his political faith, was a constant vindication of this instinct.

To some, his reasons for wishing to become one of the landed gentry of England—an object which, with the powerful support and patronage of the Bentincks, he achieved, in spite of considerable debts—will always seem so plainly associated with his political ambitions as to be, if not actually discreditable, at least slightly absurd. Yet the acquisition of the Hughenden estate was simply the final, inevitable step in a premeditated process of identifying himself with England. Like other Jews, before him and since—the Rothschilds, for example—he recognised the importance of possessing a share in the land of his adoption. Property, in his opinion, was that which entitled a man to nationality in the fullest sense of the word, and if this happened to be one of the main doctrines of the party to which, after some hesitation, he attached himself, it was also one of the most inveterate characteristics of the race from which he had sprung.

Further, it was not really inconsistent with his own character, though it is rather disconcerting to find that one whose tastes and manners at first were those of the parvenu rather than of the country squire, should have loved the calm, unpretentious scenery of the Chilterns ; that the beech groves and pines at Hughenden and the unruffled solitude of his library—the two material possessions he cared most for—could cast a deeper spell upon him than all the glitter and distinction of London society. But his most impressionable years, it should be remembered, had been spent in similar surroundings at Bradenham ; and it was in Berkshire, not in Belgravia, that he had experienced what was perhaps the strongest personal emotion of his life in his devoted attachment to his sister Sarah. It was after her death and after the death of the old antiquary, his father, that he must have felt behind his violent ambition to succeed the need for some kind of security, something to which he could return, as he had once been able to return to Bradenham when his health had broken down, and of which, if all failed, he could say : " This at least is mine."

It was in something of the same kind of spirit that he acquired as a wife the widow of the man who had been returned with him to Parliament for Maidstone in 1837. He had earlier confessed, with more assurance and less cynicism than one would expect in a young man, that he would never marry for love. There was, in fact, an awkward moment during his engagement when Mrs. Wyndham Lewis, with her substantial income and mansion in Park Lane, suspected that this was exactly what he proposed to do. The marriage, however, was surprisingly successful. It is enough that Disraeli publicly proclaimed her in the dedication to *Sybil* as " the perfect wife." In her he seems to have found, though not perhaps immediately, besides a town house and a secured income, an anchorage for his shifting, nervous sensibility ; and through her that confidence in himself, the lack of which was the chief cause of the insufferable presumption and egoism of his youth. More than that he does not seem to have required, and in return he accepted her rather painful exuberance, her vanity, and peculiar, even vulgar, tastes. Inferior to him in every respect but years—she was twelve years his senior and already middle-aged when he married her—she watched over him and cherished him for more than thirty years, preserving every word he wrote to her and even the hair which she clipped from his head regularly throughout their married life. But of passion there was none. Whether Disraeli ever felt any it is reasonable to doubt. In a somewhat ambiguous phrase, in that doubtfully autobiographical novel *Henrietta Temple*, which pretends to be a record of an early love-affair, he affirmed that " the passions that endure flash like the lightning ; they scorch the soul, but it is warmed for ever." Ambition for greatness as a writer first and then as a man of action seems to have insulated his own heart from such a dangerous charge. Passions which in a man like Lord Byron were focused upon women, in Disraeli were deflected into other channels

and were largely dissipated in the exhausting strife of
party politics. Not passion, but sympathy and encouragement were what Disraeli asked for and abun-
dantly received.

His relations with women—with his sister, his wife,
Mrs. Brydges Williams, and the two platonic mis-
tresses of his declining years, Lady Chesterfield and
her younger sister, Lady Bradford—were in the nature
of escapes from reality, and the part he played in them
was rather that of a child than a lover. He did, indeed,
stress, on more than one occasion, the spiritual at the
expense of the physical nature of his affections, and it
is certainly doubtful whether he ever needed the con-
solations of the flesh as much as he did those of the
spirit. Love was the fabric of that romantic dream-
world whose claims contrasted so oddly with those of
his political career—claims which divided his attention and as he grew older frequently interfered with
one another. "My Nature," he had proclaimed in his
youth, "demands that my life should be perpetual
love." Seven years before his death, he clinched this
boyish conceit with the words : "I owe everything to
women ; and if, in the sunset of life, I have still a
young heart, it is due to that influence." It was, in
truth, the heart of a child that had never grown up.
And like a child, with its urgent longing to be understood and appreciated, caressed and made much of,
he would often appeal through self-pity or commisera-
tion for the solace and approval he required. To
Lady Blessington he could write : "I have exposed
myself to so many griefs and am worn by so many
cares that the present always demands my energies,
and I seldom venture to indulge in memory, for the
past has too many pangs."

While it is certainly true that he suffered much from
the insolence of office and the sudden deaths of friends

and relatives, one cannot help suspecting that he was not altogether unaware, as he wrote, of the appeal of egotism cunningly displayed. This, undoubtedly, was not the least important element in his genius for clever flattery. It may be that he was consciously insincere on some occasions—his letters to the Queen after the death of the Prince Consort are embarrassingly fulsome —but in general his flattery appears to have been a well-intentioned, if insidious, method of breaking down his own and others' inhibitions and so creating an atmosphere of intimacy. Few people can resist such flattery when it is skilfully applied. It procured for Disraeli the attention, the response, and that illusion of happiness without which he must have languished. His wife, as we have seen, did all that he asked of her in this respect, clipping his hair, feeding him richly after a weary session in the House, redecorating Hughenden and furnishing it in her own distinctive way, and generally relieving him of domestic affairs, which he considered himself totally unfitted to manage. In short, he had to be made happy, and if Mary Anne, his wife, became virtually his slave, there were others no less ready to serve him. For twelve years Mrs. Brydges Williams, an elderly Jewish widow, was a kind of fairy-godmother to him. Throughout her reign, the succulent lobsters, prawns, and mullets of Torquay, the choicest blooms of the Cornish Riviera lay heaped on the tables at Hughenden and Park Lane. This friendship, so romantic and at times so sweetly sentimental, had an even more solid, material background. When the old lady died, £30,000—the bulk of her fortune—passed to Disraeli, and this noble legacy was fondly acknowledged by his granting her wish to be buried in his private vault at Hughenden.

This craving for affection, which was really all his " fiery passions " needed for their satisfaction, reached a climax in his personal relations with the Queen. The conquest of her heart was something that even his " awful ambition " can scarcely have contemplated. The death of the Prince Consort gave him an opening, and the elaborate display of sympathy he made on that dreadful occasion instantly dispelled any doubts which the Queen may have shared with her confidential advisers about Disraeli's political integrity. In the darkest days of her widowhood, she came to rely on him for consolation and advice. While he, carried away by the romantic circumstances which had placed a simple woman at the supreme head of the State, and by a semitic instinct to consolidate and extend the power and prestige of the Throne, took endless pains to soften with soothing flattery the pangs of her inordinate grief ; to restore her self-confidence by subtle submission to her whims, and to give her an erroneous conception of her importance by deferring at every step to her formidable personality. In explanation of his method of dealing with her, he would remark diplomatically : " I never deny ; I never contradict ; I sometimes forget."

As the relations of monarch and minister slipped by smooth and easy stages into friendship, and from friendship into affection, Disraeli realised that Society had nothing more to offer him. Birth, Beauty, Wealth no longer appealed with their dazzling and seductive charms to one who had broken through the prejudice and rigid conventions of the English aristocracy and been entertained at Blenheim, Hatfield, and Knowsley ; to one who had eaten ham with Louis Philippe and been nearly overturned in a skiff by Louis Napoleon—and who, when the same prince had become Emperor, triumphed in the cosmopolitan salons of Paris under the Second Empire.

In the summer of the year 1868 Royal favour ex-

pressed itself for the first time in flowers, and thence-
forward these gifts, which have done more than anything else to commemorate the Queen's affection for
her first minister, regularly perfumed the endless letters
and tender messages with which they were usually
accompanied. In 1876, at a moment when public
opinion had turned against him on account of his
wavering policy in regard to the Bulgarian atrocities,
he was elevated to the Peerage, as Viscount Hughenden
and Earl of Beaconsfield. A year later the Queen,
who had done much in her turn to mitigate Disraeli's
loneliness after the death of his wife in 1872, lunched
with him at Hughenden; and it was shortly after this
that her host, by then very infirm and asthmatic, wrote
to her that " during a somewhat romantic and imaginative life, nothing had ever occurred to him so interesting as this confidential correspondence with one so
exalted and inspiring." It is unnecessary to adorn the
tale with details of the exchange of portraits and
bibelots, the offers of dukedoms and marquisates,
which she made and he delicately refused, and the
Garter, which crowned Disraeli's victory at the Congress of Berlin, when unfortunately he was too old
and ill to appreciate either victory or its rewards. The
marble tablet, which his " Faery Queen " ordered to
be placed in the chancel of Hughenden church after
his death, speaks for itself :

To THE DEAR AND HONOURED MEMORY OF

BENJAMIN, EARL OF BEACONSFIELD,

THIS MEMORIAL IS PLACED BY HIS
GRATEFUL SOVEREIGN AND FRIEND,
VICTORIA R.I.
" Kings love him that speaketh right."

But the last eight years of his romantic and imaginative life were occupied by other equally " interesting "

attachments. At the age of seventy, he was able to say, " I have lived to know the twilight of love has its splendour and richness." And again—rather pathetically—" When you have the government of a country on your shoulders, to *love* a person, and to be *in love* with a person makes all the difference." The cause of this strange emotional outburst was Selina, Countess of Bradford, and a contributory cause her elder sister by nearly twenty years, the septuagenarian and widowed Countess of Chesterfield. A year after his wife's death, which deprived him not only of domestic bliss but of the mansion in Park Lane and a large part of his income as well, Disraeli renewed his acquaintance with these two old ladies, who had faded out of his life for nearly half a century. In the manner of Horace Walpole to the two Miss Berrys, he poured out to them his most secret hopes and fears ; his difficulties with the Queen, not only over the major issues of State, but in such matters as the humane slaughtering of young seals and the recovery of a Lady-in-Waiting's stolen jewellery ; his admiration and concern for the Prince of Wales ; and the unbearable agony of a solitary existence. A return of the old longing for sympathy and compassion carried him, old as he was, to the most extraordinary lengths. His visits to Lady Bradford soon became embarrassing in their frequency and inappropriateness. With pride he admitted how " in the midst of stately councils " he found time to scribble notes to her and to her sister and boasted that he employed official messengers to deliver them. In the early stages of this fanciful romance, his letters—and there were to be 1,600 of them, all told—explore every shade of feeling, from the raptures of the most ecstatic delight to the depths of the most abysmal despair. Gay, witty, flirtatious, despondent, complaining, jealous, thwarted, forgiving, he could say, within two years of Mary Anne's death, and not-withstanding an acute attack of gout : " I have reached the pinnacle of power and gauged the deepest affec-tions of ye heart." Such moments, alas! were rare. Usually when the " wild thought " that he might still become " an object of concentrated feeling " seemed to be on the very point of consummation, something would happen to dash him to earth. " If the person I most love," he wrote on such an occasion, " is false or deficient to me in thought or feeling, I experience sufferings which neither Bismarck nor Gortchakoff could inflict on me." In a moment of calm he paused to sum up the curious situation he had created :

" I am certain there is no greater misfortune than to have a heart that will not grow old. It requires all the sternness of public life to sustain one. If we have to govern a great country, we ought not to be distrait and feel the restlessness of love. Such things should be the appanage of the youthful heroes I have so often painted. But alas! I always drew from my own ex-perience, and were I to write again to-morrow, I fear I should be able to do justice to the most agitating, though the most amiable weakness of humanity."

The violent excitement of the early letters subsided as increasing complications in the European situation of the late 'seventies and growing infirmities claimed more and more of his failing strength. But though he was thwarted of his heart's desire, at least he derived a certain amount of happiness from the rare country visits he found time to pay to Lady Bradford at Weston and Lady Chesterfield at Bretby ; and even if he had to admit that he was not loved as much as he believed himself to be in love, he consoled himself with the knowledge that he was at any rate cherished and admired. For all this, he felt very keenly the isolation to which his soaring ambitions had finally carried him ;

the lonely elevation he had reached in politics was no compensation for, but rather intensified, the solitude of his private life. " I want and welcome public toil," he lamented, " for my sources of private happiness are very slight and not very satisfactory." There is significance in the fact that he disliked the company of his own sex ; " I hate clubs," he said, " not being fond of male society." Probably he realised that with his demonstrative, emotional temperament he could never hope to melt the frigid reserve of the well-bred Englishman. To such men, with their characteristic intransigeance and unwillingness to accept anything out of the common, Disraeli was always a foreigner. " The impenetrable man " was Bishop Wilberforce's comment ; Carlyle, in a generous moment, called him " a superlative Hebrew conjuror." That he might have anything in common with them outside politics was out of the question, so true it is that the heart far more than the home is an Englishman's castle ! Success, as it always will, had gained for him admission to the home, but was to deny him for ever access to the heart ; respected and often admired and sometimes even worshipped by his colleagues, he was never really loved. If this is true of men like Lord George Bentinck, Lord Derby, and his secretary Montague Corry, with whom he worked in the closest possible intimacy, it is more markedly so in the attitude of such a statesman as Lord Salisbury. The nearest he ever came to an intimate relation with men was with two other foreigners—the Prince Consort and Louis Philippe.

The most striking feature of Disraeli's career is the impact of his feminine nature on politics. It revealed itself in his inability to pay attention to accuracy and detail ; in his dangerous and unreliable faculty for grasping the key to a situation by intuition, rather

than by the use of reason ; in his romantic conception of the sovereign and her empire, which was
harshly criticised when the Act to confer the title of
Empress of India on the Queen was presented to
Parliament ; and not least of all in his heroine worship
of the Queen herself. Yet, in spite of his exceptional
capacity for hard work, which was only surpassed by
that of his great adversary, Gladstone, his nature fulfilled itself in the dreams rather than in the achievements of statesmanship. The visionary and the man
of action wrestled within him continually. Out of his
dreams of " a Real Throne " and " Imperium et
Libertas " singularly little emerged—except possibly
the Queen. They certainly had the good effect of
drawing her out of her prolonged widowhood and back
from her endless excursions on the Continent ; to
Disraeli she owed, at least, the restoration of her
long-lost popularity.

It is true that by a brilliant stroke he acquired a
controlling share for his country in the management of
the Suez Canal ; that from the hesitations and bloody
confusions which ended in his triumphal progress to the
Congress of Berlin, where the extravagant rococo of
Sans Souci and the Neues Palace revived for a moment
his earliest enthusiasms, he produced Cyprus and the
notorious and specious catchword, " Peace with Honour " ; but the record of his thirteen years as leader
of the Conservative Party, which he had done so much
to consolidate after the apostasy of Peel, is for the most
part one of unfulfilled ambitions in foreign affairs, of a
perpetual struggle against obstructions at home and
abroad, of endless debates on minor points of domestic
reform, ending in Gladstone's triumphal Midlothian
campaign and the defeat of the Conservative Government almost exactly a year before its leader's death.

This year was to be one of increasing suffering for

Disraeli, aggravated by the excessive strain of his last six years in office. " Ah," he complained, " when one has got everything in the world one ever wished for and is prostrate with pain or debility, one knows the value of health, which one never could comprehend in the days of youth and love." But in retirement at Hughenden, broken only by the tiresome necessity of winter journeys to London to attend divisions in the House of Lords, he yet had strength to finish another novel—*Endymion*—in which he expressed in its fullest form his conviction that woman exercises an immense influence in moulding a man's life and particularly his political career. It was the final round in the lifelong conflict between the romantic and the man of action.

In society, which clamoured still for his company, he withdrew further and further into himself and his own dreams. Silent, brooding, and impassive, he seemed deaf to its siren voice, oblivious of its charms. The world, he knew, was changing ; the influence and renown of the aristocracy, which had once meant so much to him, were slowly waning. With failing eyes he watched—aloof, mysterious, sphinx-like—the passing of the old order of things. In the House of Lords, as in his later days in the Commons, he became fixed in a kind of ozymandian immobility, from which even the taunts of his opponents seldom roused him. Was this also a pose—contrasting so strangely with the insolent, flashy, and incalculable tactics by which as a young man he had stormed his way into the world ? The secret was never given away. Silence—unfathomable, inexplicable—enveloped his thoughts and feelings in a veil of mystery.

There were those who remembered an incident at an evening party when, placing a finger on the arm of a young beauty, he had murmured a single word . . . Canova ! And there are others, still living, who, look-

ing back over more than half a century, can still recall
to mind a bent figure gliding like a shadow through
the dim corridors and lobbies of Westminster ; some,
too, who have vivid memories of a face, made, so it
seemed to their childish fancy, of wax or old parch-
ment, of a forefinger lifting a drooping eyelid from an
eye that gave one rapid gleam and then seemed to
grow dim, of lips that slowly shaped themselves to kiss,
kissed, and became once again part of an embittered
wistful countenance. " What a strange thing is life ! "
he wrote in his old age, " and what a stranger thing
the human heart ! I can decipher neither, though in
my time I was once thought a judge of that sort of
thing." By then his early taste for speculation had
been dulled in politics, which cares only for temporal
problems and has neither time nor inclination for the
eternal. He seems to have recognised this when he
wrote to Lady Bradford : " The page of human life
is quickly read, and one does not care to dwell upon
it, unless it touches the heart."

The statesmen of one generation are so soon forgotten by those of the next that after fifty years their
policies, their failures, and successes are scarcely dis-
tinguishable except by the curious in the smooth
pattern of history. " Reflect on things past, as wars,
negotiations, factions, etc. We enter so little into those
interests, that we wonder how men could possibly be
so busy and concerned for things so transitory ; look
on the present times, we find the same humour, yet
wonder not at all." But whatever we may think of
Disraeli as a statesman—and the younger generation
of to-day, putting its political faith, if any, in Communism or Fascism, probably thinks very little—the fascination of his character and personality is endlessly
absorbing. The vanity of many of his schemes, in
particular his policy of imperialism, is apparent in a

world that is ruled, not by kings and emperors, least of all by one King-Emperor, but by economic necessity.

No statesman has ever shown more clearly than Disraeli did in his novels and letters the loneliness and emptiness of a life spent in public service. To most servants of the State, service is its own reward and provides all the satisfaction their ambitions and vanities require. But Disraeli needed something more than the fame which he ultimately won, something, half-glimpsed in dreams which vanished in the business of the day—an explanation of the mystery of life. For he alone amongst his great contemporaries remained incurably romantic in a utilitarian age. Neither the mullets of Torquay nor the primroses of Osborne ever wholly satisfied his lofty aspirations. Even the trim terraces and wooded walks at Hughenden, which became so much a part of himself, were themselves part of that England which, though it had adopted him, never returned his affection and devotion in full.

PAUL EHRLICH

BY MARGARET GOLDSMITH

PAUL EHRLICH

PAUL EHRLICH

By Margaret Goldsmith

THERE is no German, no European, in fact, who has had a more far-reaching civic influence on our century that Dr. Paul Ehrlich, the great bacteriologist, who discovered Salvarsan, more popularly known as " 606," a remedy against syphilis. By helping to stamp out the most terrible of diseases, Ehrlich made more than a theoretical contribution to science. His work points the way to scientific discoveries which will ultimately result in an improvement of public health and thus a regeneration of mankind. Many famous inventions have been named after the men of genius who made them, but this German Jew was too modest, too much absorbed by the work itself, to immortalise his own name in connection with his scientific achievement. In common with most really great men he was far too busy, up to the very day of his death in 1915, to bother about what the world at large thought of him, or whether he was personally remembered by later generations.

His manner was so simple and unassuming that few people meeting him, except the colleagues familiar with his work, realised the distinctions that had been heaped upon him. The German *Who's Who* for 1914 lists over thirty honorary degrees and decorations given him by foreign countries and universities. He was a foreign member of the Royal Society, an honorary member of the Society of Tropical Medicine, a Doctor of Science of Oxford ; he had been decorated by the Russian, the Spanish, the Danish, and other European Governments. In this connection it is interesting to note that from Germany, his own country, he had

received only the Order of the Red Eagle *Third* Class.
For in pre-War Germany there was, at least, a social
boycott of the Jews and first-class honours were with-
held from them, both in the academic world and in
public life. And Ehrlich remained a loyal Jew to his
death. Many of his fellow-believers were baptized for
reasons. of expediency or ambition, but he clung
tenaciously to his faith and to his race.

By temperament, too, he remained an outsider. He
could never take himself quite as seriously as most
German professors do, and his sense of humour included himself and his own idiosyncrasies. He made
fun, for instance, of his peculiar passion for popular
music. Was it not odd, he admitted, for a serious
scientist to be stimulated by tunes such as the *Merry
Widow* waltz, which his wife or one of his two daughters
played for him literally for hours as he sat reading or
thinking ?

Ehrlich was never pompous, never conscious of his
own importance. With large spectacles, a neat beard,
kindly eyes, questioning to the point of sadness, a
sympathetic mouth, and a high forehead, he super-
ficially resembled many doctors of his generation.
Actually, however, he was less and less like them as
he grew older. He had no feeling for professional
propriety, so highly developed in the German upper
middle classes before the War. He had no understanding of that cult of the *Standesgemäss*, of what a
man in a certain station in life may or may not do
with dignity. He had no social ambition. " I hate
associating with pundits (social gatherings where one
is supposed to feel honoured)," he once wrote to his
daughter, " and I hate parties given merely because
the people attending may be useful to each other."
He lived up to these principles, associating with any
man, no matter how humble, if this man had some-

thing to give him intellectually. He was not interested in his friends' grandparents, long since in their graves, or in the honours they or their relations had received from the Kaiser or others in authority. In this lack of snobbishness, Ehrlich was not a Prussian in the pre-War meaning of the word.

Many of his serious associates, for ever conscious of the dignity of their profession, and thus of the respect due to their persons, heartily disapproved of his democratic manner. At the Robert Koch Institute, with which Ehrlich was informally connected for several years, some of his colleagues were seriously shocked because often—that is to say whenever he felt like it—he drank a mug of beer with his laboratory assistants. And his laboratory was never tidy. Papers, periodicals in many languages, and unanswered letters were strewn about the chairs, the window ledges, and even the floor. Rarely was Ehrlich seen without a fat cigar in his mouth. He smoked incessantly, and the stuffy air of his workrooms increased the general atmosphere of confusion. This outward untidiness was the more annoying to his associates, because his careful results forced them to admit that his mind was never disorderly or vague. He surpassed most of them in his experimental exactitude ; he was infinitely painstaking, and his scientific imagination, which amounted to genius, never impaired his passion for detail. " We fail chiefly because we fail to be exact," he once wrote.

If the superiority of his mind had not annoyed some members of the German medical profession of his day, his outward untidiness would not have troubled them. But he thought so much more quickly than they did, that they were often filled with a feeling of inferiority. His imagination leapt ahead of the minds of his German contemporaries, who built up their theories slowly, step by step. And often his sense of humour bewildered, or even offended them. His undaunted optimism furthermore irritated many people, as optimism in the face of apparently insurmountable difficulties so often does. Number 606 will indicate, for instance, how many remedies Ehrlich prepared in his laboratory before he finally achieved his ultimate success.

Another thing that made some of his medical colleagues suspicious of him was his versatility, for the majority of them were men of one-track minds, a type not uncommon amongst professors anywhere, especially in Germany. To be a real expert, they believed, you must close your mind to everything but one special line of work. Ehrlich was mistrusted by a considerable group of biologists because he did not stick to one subject and one subject only. Throughout his life he was haunted by a restless curiosity ; his mind was constantly reaching out to discover and investigate new fields for scientific adventure. He was an insatiable reader. He was interested in every phase of medicine, pathology, and chemistry, apart from biology, which became his absorbing passion.

.   .   .   .

Paul Ehrlich was born on March 14, 1854, in Strehlen, a small town near Breslau in Silesia, where to-day, ironically enough, considering what this man has done for the purification of the German race, the persecution of the Jews is more relentless than in almost any other part of Germany. His father, Isma Ehrlich, was a simple, kindly man of business, but his mother, a woman of unusual imagination, was determined that her son, whose talents she early recognised, was to have a university education. The boy was sent to the Mary Magdalen Gymnasium in Breslau, where he dutifully passed his matriculation examinations, but where he won no distinctions. He was never considered a brilliant scholar, for he was frankly bored with the school routine, devoting his real energies to outside subjects and reading. His conventional schoolmasters were distressed by his wandering imagination. They demanded Prussian discipline of their pupils and a concentration on the subjects prescribed by the accepted curriculum.

Many of his relatives—and one can imagine what argumentative conferences were held about this boy in his large Jewish family—urged Ehrlich's parents to give up their plan for his higher education. But his mother persisted, and as soon as he had left the Gymnasium he entered the school of medicine at the University of Breslau. Here young Ehrlich was extremely fortunate, for he studied under some of the most distinguished German medical men of the day. He attended lectures by Julius Cohnheim, the great experimental pathologist, and by Karl Weigert, known in medicine for his investigations of smallpox and Bright's disease. Ehrlich was particularly impressed and stimulated by the work of another of his professors, Rudolf Heidenhain, whose experiments in staining kidney-cells by injecting indigo-carmine into the blood were rousing great interest at the time.

Ehrlich puzzled many of his professors. He was generally considered a very mediocre student, a young man apparently without the slightest interest in theoretical medicine. It was with an obvious effort that he forced himself to memorise the names of the bones and muscles of the bodies he dissected ; he crammed, without enthusiasm, for tests and examinations. He never showed a competitive spirit ; he had no desire to distinguish himself among his fellow-students. He seemed more keen about chemistry than he was about medicine. In common with Paracelsus, the great seventeenth-century physician, who helped emancipate medical science from the superstitions of alchemy, Ehrlich, even as a student, believed that there must be a chemical specific for the cure of every disease. Ehrlich himself often referred to his own " chemical imagination."

Despite his apparently wild ideas, his lack of concentration on the prescribed studies, all of his professors, though some of them grudgingly, were forced to admit that there was some intangible quality about Ehrlich's approach to medicine which showed an unusually inquiring mind. He would either, so they decided amongst themselves, be a very great success or a complete failure. None of them guessed that his greatest talent would one day be for theoretical medicine, for research. But they left him alone to pursue the queer microscopical experiments which seemed to absorb him entirely. He was frequently observed fussing about with his slides and staining tissues with strange dye-stuffs, usually methylene blue. As far as his instructors could see, his seemingly aimless experiments had little, if anything, to do with the course outlined by the faculty of medicine.

But at the Universities of Strassburg and Leipzig and Freiburg—for Paul Ehrlich was a restless young man who disliked staying in one place—his professors began to take him more seriously. They soon realised that in his independent researches, his " fiddling " with his microscope, he had actually been investigating the symptoms of lead poisoning. And he had found that those organs of the animals which had been most affected by the poison while the animal was still alive were most sensitive to lead, even after they were later removed from the animal's body. This made him speculate about the chemical affinity between animal tissues and foreign bodies generally.

These revolutionary conjectures led him directly to his first great discovery : certain dye-stuffs, he startled his professor by announcing, as well as lead, clung to the animal tissues. And if these tissues could be coloured, and thus stand out under the microscopic lens, the study of tissues and their diseases would be infinitely simplified. His application of aniline dye-stuffs to tissues, now known to biology as " triacid stains," was immediately acknowledged as a very practical and important contribution to medical research.

While he was still a student, furthermore, he became greatly interested in the morphology of the blood. During these investigations he improved the methods of drying blood-smears on microscope slides by heat. He found that certain cells, which he called " mast cells," granulated when dyed with basic aniline dyes. His professors no longer wondered whether he would be a success or a failure ; their puzzled curiosity about him had changed to a very real respect. And his doctor's thesis, " Contribution to the Theory and Practice of Histological Colouring," was read with interest not only by his examiners at Breslau, where he had returned in 1878 to qualify as a physician, but by members of the medical profession throughout Germany.

It was no wonder, therefore, that this promising young man attracted the attention of Friedrich Theodor Frerichs, the most noted German clinician of the day and one of the founders of experimental pathology. Frerichs, who was the chief medical officer of the Charité Hospital in Berlin, invited Ehrlich to join his staff. The next seven or eight years were one of the most fruitful and satisfying periods of Ehrlich's life. He was now happily married to Hedwig Pinkus, the daughter of a Silesian industrialist, and his chief, Dr. Frerichs, who had a profound understanding of his young assistant's unusual talents, gave him a free hand in the Charité laboratories. Ehrlich worked steadily and well during these peaceful years, chiefly on research into the blood. With the help of his now famous method of staining, he succeeded in dividing the white blood corpuscles into what doctors call the neutrophilic, the basophilic, and the oxyphilic. To-day the investigation of various kinds of white blood cells forms a part of the routine work in every hospital ward, and this has been made possible by Ehrlich's pioneer work in hæmatology.

While at the Charité, Ehrlich also found new ways of diagnosing typhoid fever. He was furthermore studying pernicious anæmia. Recognition for his research in so many fields of medicine was not lacking. Frerichs, like Ehrlich himself, was more than generous about giving his assistants full credit for their original work. In 1884 Ehrlich was granted the title of Professor by the Prussian Ministry of Education—an honour never before conferred on any physician who was not, at the same time, a teacher at some university.

When Frerichs died a year later, Ehrlich experienced his first serious disappointment. Dr. Carl Gerhardt, who succeeded Frerichs at the Charité, was a literal-minded, jealous man. Unless he could see immediate results, he thought that his assistants were wasting their time. Ehrlich was given a great deal of purely routine work to do and had little time for research. His rounds of the hospital wards tired him. He was always far more interested in discovering the causes of diseases than in healing an individual patient. He never claimed to be a successful practitioner. " I believe," he once declared, " that progress in the understanding of disease can only be brought about by a theoretical point of view and that a misguided theory is more fruitful than crude empirical experience, which merely registers facts without explanations."

The routine work under Gerhardt, this curtailment of his freedom, was particularly irksome to him, as in 1882 he had heard Robert Koch lecture on his final discovery of the tubercle bacillus—" the most gripping experience of my scientific life," he later confessed. Always indefatigable, Ehrlich yearned, apart from his other interests, to do some work on the study of tuberculosis. And he succeeded, despite his nagging duties at the hospital, for it was he who discovered that tubercle bacilli are acid-fast, but that they could be stained with fuchsine dye. Again he facilitated the microscopical study of a disease, thus making a real contribution to the practical application of Koch's discovery.

It was not a simple matter for Paul Ehrlich to resign from his post at the Charité. As a Jew, appointments at State research institutions were closed to him, as were full professorships at universities. Probably no one who is not a scientist himself can understand what this boycott meant to him, for the State institutions controlled all the laboratories which were really well equipped ; only full professors could freely use the university laboratories. If a Jewish scientist succeeded beyond a certain point despite these tremendous technical disadvantages it was obvious that he must be a man not only of unusual gifts but of remarkable character as well.

Obviously Ehrlich was such a man. Had he, at this time, submitted to a formal baptism, become a member of the Protestant Church, his scientific future would have been a simple matter. But, curious as this may seem considering his passion for his work, his loyalty to his race and to his religion was stronger even than his scientific urge. His feeling of solidarity with his race was an unalterable part of himself.

In 1887, therefore, this man, who had been granted an honorary, though quite meaningless, professorship, installed himself at the University of Berlin as a *Privat Dozent*, an unpaid lecturer who was permitted to teach at the university, but who was given only the dues paid by the students for his particular courses. He was not, in other words, on the list of established professors. Unless they were Jews, German university teachers accepted these posts only at the very beginning of their careers. A *Privat Dozent* was really on trial, a man not yet accepted as an instructor of any reputation or importance.

Naturally Ehrlich's lectures were crowded, but he was dissatisfied and worried, run down after his years of friction with pompous Dr. Gerhardt. In 1888 Ehrlich fell ill : a tuberculous infection caught in his laboratory. He was sent to Egypt, where he was forced to spend over a year. Here he made a complete recovery ; his lungs never gave him any trouble again. And the enforced solitude, the leisure to think and to read, had caused his normal optimism to reassert itself. When he returned to Germany late in 1889 his old fighting spirit, his indomitable buoyancy had been completely re-established.

Philosophically facing the fact that Government laboratories were closed to him, and this *Verbot* included Koch's new Institute for Infectious Diseases in Berlin, Ehrlich calmly decided to open a small laboratory of his own. Fortunately for him, his wife, who was almost as interested in his work as he was himself, was not without private means, and so he rented two small rooms on the ground floor of a house in Steglitz, a suburb of Berlin. Here he worked for over a year. He plunged deeply into new investigations of dye-stuffs and their effects on animal tissues, and in this laboratory in Steglitz he did the basic work on his *Farbenanalyse*, which established him as the pioneer in the analysis of dye-stuffs.

In his little workrooms in Steglitz he began also to consider the whole problem of immunity against diseases in general and against vegetable poisons in particular. These conjectures later developed into his picturesque " Side Chain Theory of Immunity." He tried to prove a fantastic notion that the living protoplasmic molecules inaking up the human body consist of an unchanging centre, or nucleus, and of a changing periphery, or " side chain." The latter, so he hoped to prove, combine chemically with various poisons, thus neutralising them. This was the only flight of Ehrlich's imagination which had no foundation in reality. His side chain theory has been generally disproved. Though these researches were in themselves futile, his methods, even in this aimless quest, bore practical fruits. Without them, as August von Wassermann himself admitted, his own diagnosis and the now famous Wassermann test for syphilis could never have been established. August von Wassermann many years later called Ehrlich's investigations of immunity " a staff with which to gain a firm foothold in the moving quicksands of opinion."

While Ehrlich was working quietly in his laboratory in Steglitz—this was in 1890—a tremendous event occurred in the medical world. At the Tenth International Medical Congress, held in Berlin, Robert Koch announced to the world that he had discovered a remedy against tuberculosis. He himself emphasised that his new medicine, tuberculin, would cure the disease only in its early stages, but many of his medical contemporaries joined the lay world in hailing his new medicine as the cure for all cases. This disease, so

some enthusiasts declared, was now a terror of the past.
The newspapers were full of Koch's great contribution ;
his discovery roused a popular interest in the tremendous progress medicine had been making in the nineteenth century. Pasteur and Koch, Roux and Yersin,
all of these scientists sprang into the news.

Interested journalists, as well as medical men, began
to wonder what had happened to Paul Ehrlich, who had
done such remarkable work as Frerichs' assistant at
the Charité. Robert Koch felt that he himself, and
medical research in general, could no longer do without
the co-operation of this distinguished Jew. The anti-
Semitic traditions of Prussia made it impossible for
Koch to appoint Ehrlich as one of his regular assistants
at the Institute for Infectious Diseases, but a man as
clever as Koch soon found a way out : Ehrlich was
not asked to become an official member of the staff
at the Institute, but a special laboratory, special
assistants and equipment were provided for him at
the Moabit Hospital, still one of Berlin's most famous
clinics. Here he co-operated with Koch on an in-
formal basis. At the same time, through Koch's influence, Ehrlich was appointed an " extraordinary
professor " at the University of Berlin, an appointment but one rank below that of full professor, and
the highest rank open to a Jew. Even Einstein, except
for a brief period during the German Republic, was
never more than an *ausserordentlicher* professor.

Ehrlich's association with Robert Koch continued
for six years. Ehrlich studied tuberculin, proving
by his experiments that only a very gradual injec-
tion of increasingly large quantities of the anti-tuber-
culous toxin was really effective. He assisted Koch
in his fight against the terrible cholera epidemic which
broke out in Hamburg in 1892 ; he was keenly
interested in Koch's work on infections caused by

drinking impure water. No matter how great the burden of his independent investigations, his interest in other scientific work never flagged. During these years he was doing some of his own most important research. He improved Behring's anti-toxin for diphtheria, he introduced methylene-blue as a cure for quartan fever, and he was now absorbed by cancer research. For years he worked practically in the dark, but with infinite perseverance. Later, after Nicolas Jensen, the great Danish biologist, had developed cancer research to a more modern science, Ehrlich's researches facilitated the diagnosis of the disease.

Even Ehrlich's most jealous, or most anti-Semitic, colleagues could no longer overlook his outstanding achievements. Obviously the time had come when his relatively confined workrooms in the Moabit Hospital were too small, when it was apparent to every scientist in Germany that it would be a loss to medicine if he were not provided with a larger scope for his activities. The study of serums launched by Pasteur was fast developing into a separate scientific field. Biologists everywhere were at work in their laboratories trying to discover the immune properties of various serums. Obviously Ehrlich's contribution to serology was essential. In the end it was not his fellow-scientists, however, who nagged the Prussian State authorities, the Treasury and the Institute for Public Health until, at last, an exception was made in Ehrlich's case and a special institute was founded for his work. In 1896 Althoff, a civil servant, the director of high schools and universities in Prussia, and Adicke, the Mayor of Frankfort on the Main, both of them staunch supporters of Ehrlich, finally persuaded the Government to found a " provisional " Institute for Serum Research and Serum Investigation, which Ehrlich was to direct. This Institute was opened in

Steglitz, near Berlin, where he had maintained his own small laboratories. This "provisional" clause gave the Government a loophole. Anti-Semitic elements could be assured that the position held by Ehrlich, a Jew, was not a permanent civil service appointment.

A few years later, in 1899, an Institute for Experimental Therapy was founded in Frankfurt, where Ehrlich's discoveries were to be carried farther. Ehrlich left his "provisional" work and moved to Frankfurt. He was now forty-five years old. Already he had done invaluable service to science. Had he died then he would have been remembered as a famous man. Actually, however, he did his most important work, made his greatest contributions to science after he was fifty. And work in Frankfurt became easier as the years passed, for, thanks to the interest of the Speyer family in scientific progress, he had almost unlimited funds and laboratories at his disposal. "The Georg Speyer Haus for Chemotherapy," founded by Frau Fransica Speyer, the widow of Georg Speyer, the banker, in 1906, became the centre of his personal investigations.

He never neglected any of his many lines of investigation. Late in the 'nineties, for instance, he published his well-known thesis on anæmia, he showed an active interest in Alphonse Laveran's discovery of the malaria parasite ; but from the time he moved to Frankfurt he concentrated his major energies on investigating the causes and cures of venereal diseases. The modern history of syphilis is, in fact, bound up with the work of three great German scientists : Wassermann, Schaudinn, and Ehrlich. In 1905 Schaudinn discovered the spirochete causing the disease ; in 1906 Wassermann discovered the test for ascertaining its presence, and in 1910 Ehrlich found the cure which is still the basis of the therapeutics of this scourge.

For over ten years Ehrlich worked with inexhaustible patience on this, his greatest discovery. Alphonse Laveran, who also discovered the malaria parasite, had been working for some time on a minute animal called the trypanosome, first discovered in rats by Lewis in 1878. It was then that Fritz Schaudinn began to wonder whether the spirochete of syphilis, too, was not a tiny animal organism, unrelated to bacteria, but closely resembling trypanosomes. Ehrlich snatched at this conjecture : if he could kill trypanosomes he should be able to kill spirochetes. And it was natural that in his long campaign against the trypanosomes he used arsenic compounds, for long before his time some strong poison, such as mercury, had been used as a remedy against venereal disease. With the progress of chemistry, scientists now combined arsenic as a drug with other poisonous and non-poisonous chemicals, for arsenic alone was so strong that, though it might cure the disease, it did great harm to the patient as well. Even a new remedy, Atoxyl, discovered during Ehrlich's time, which was used for sleeping sickness, skin diseases and anæmia, could not be applied in sufficiently strong doses to counteract syphilis. Inexperienced physicians who had experimented with this medicine soon discovered that their patients' nervous systems, chiefly the optic nerves, were atrophied by its application.

The task Ehrlich had set for himself, even if it took hundreds and hundreds of mice and rabbits, years of his time, was to discover a chemical combination with arsenic which would kill the spirochetes and yet not endanger the patient's health in other ways. He was determined to discover the proper compound of arsenic which would wipe out the parasite and yet not in-

juriously affect the tissues in the patient's body. Many
compounds succeeded in killing the spirochete in the
test-tubes, but failed when applied to animals used in
:he laboratory. Ehrlich's experiments were not unlike
the more modern use of gold salts as a remedy against
tubercle bacilli. The bacilli are killed in the test-tubes,
but attempts to apply the gold salts clinically have so
far failed to fulfil their therapeutic promise.

Ehrlich made up hundreds of compounds—605, to
be exact—before he was successful. "Arsanil," "Ars-
acetin," "Arsenophenylglycin"—he tried hundreds
of compounds, each for months and months at a time.
But always they were too strong or too weak. The
bacilli were killed, but so were the mice; or both
remained alive.

Not until 1910 did Ehrlich, with the help of his
Japanese assistant, Hata, finally stumble upon the
proper chemical combination. "606" it was called
for short; its real name is almost unspellable:
Dioxydiamidoarsenobenzol. He formally announced
his discovery at the Medical Congress in Königsberg
in 1910. But even then he could not sink back and
rest, exalted by his scientific triumph. Before his
remedy could be given over to the medical profession
for general use, tremendous difficulties had to be
overcome. Ehrlich found, for instance, that "606"
oxidised more quickly than he had anticipated, and
that in this process of oxidation the poison content of
the remedy increased rapidly, thus throwing out the
proper proportions. When it was kept in physicians'
surgeries, in other words, it changed its composition.
And there were other problems. If the water used
in the preparation of the remedy had been sterilised
some time before, there was always the danger that
the toxic remains of the bacteria in the water might
have harmful effects on the patient.

And so it was that, even after his great discovery had been made—and no drug has since been found comparable to the action of " 606 "—Ehrlich's work was not really over. But his nervous energy was not exhausted even then. He went on and on ; his task, as far as he was concerned, was not completed until, a few years later, these minor technical problems had been solved as well. He gave his assistants full credit, but he never made them do the work he had set himself.

He was equally conscientious in the use of the remedy after the technical difficulties connected with its use had been overcome. At first he permitted it to be used only under his own personal supervision. " 606 " was at first made only in the Georg Speyer Institute by his own assistants. The records of all cases were submitted to him personally. " 606 " was not distributed freely ; doctors whose ability he knew and trusted had to get it from his own laboratories. His job was never finished. . He was overworking terribly and nothing could stop him. He died of overwork in 1915.

Emil von Behring, the discoverer of anti-toxin for diphtheria, said at Ehrlich's funeral : " None of us has done as much original work as you ; you are the *magister mundi* in medical science."

JACOB EPSTEIN
BY JOHN BETJEMAN

JACOB EPSTEIN

JACOB EPSTEIN

By John Betjeman

Ever since he first made his public appearance in 1907, Jacob Epstein has been accused of blasphemy, immorality, obscenity, sensationalism, perversion, delighting in ugliness, breaking the Ten Commandments, breaking the conventions, incompetence, decadence, adultery, treachery, lack of patriotism, and many others of the major crimes which it is possible to commit in the present state of society. Though these accusations may not have increased in volume, they have not decreased in vociferousness, so that now the man-in-the-street, if he does not, like Lord Darling, confuse Epstein with Einstein, considers him to be the sort of person it is not safe to leave children alone with nor even to go near himself. You may be sure of one thing, Epstein is rarely considered as a sculptor. This is largely due to the fact that people are not interested in sculpture. They find it as uninteresting as its sister art, architecture. The art critics and the collectors and the intellectuals have made it a sort of hidden professional secret. You have to " understand " it. But there is no " understanding " about it. If you have eyes you can see it. It merely depends on how you look at it. So I imagine that an article on Epstein in a book of this sort, which contains characters so diverse, will be most useful if it merely suggests an outlook on the artist's work, and thereby his life and character.

Primarily Epstein is a Jew and proud of it. But unlike so many Jews who assimilate the customs and æsthetic standards of the country of their adoption, Epstein has chosen to get his inspiration from Jewry.

The word " Jewish " when used in connection with art, and particularly architecture, suggests a certain flamboyance and garishness with which we associate the interiors of cheap restaurants, an exaggeration of the mannerisms of the age in clothes, colour and decoration. Epstein, however, has not been imitative ; his Jewish blood has stood him in good stead, for his sculpture has an Old Testament quality that is a change from the Græco-Roman efforts of Royal Academicians. This Biblical quality is, moreover, indigenous to him and his race, a more genuine source of inspiration than could be Greek or Roman sculpture to an Englishman. Yet we were told by the popular press that Epstein was blasphemous when he made Christ a beardless Jew. Certainly Epstein has been influenced by Rodin, African sculpture and Cubism ; but they have been a means to an end : they have given the finish to his amazingly accomplished technique. They have not been his inspiration. Jewry has made him a poet.

To the casual observer, you may take it that he is a normal man, with an impressive appearance, unaffected manners, a delightful gift of conversation, and an utter indifference to public opinion or to the opinion of art critics. He is far too busy to bother about either.

That is an unusual thing about Epstein's life and character : he is a sculptor and he is busy. Despite the strong wave of public feeling against him, Epstein has his loyal supporters, and he has executed busts of characters so far apart as Lady Gregory and Admiral Lord Fisher. We have all heard of sculptors who were so poor that they had to steal stone from quarries and run away with it in a wheelbarrow by night. But Epstein, though he had not had an affluent career, has had the support of the few people in this country

who are interested in sculpture. And so the abuse
that has been showered on him has only gone to
strengthen the loyalty of those who support him. Perhaps, you, reader, will be interested in sculpture if you
go to look at the work of Epstein in the right frame
of mind. So let my opening words be the advice of
Epstein's greatest and earliest champion, the late
T. E. Hulme : " I make this very hurried protest
in the hope that I may induce those people who have
perhaps been prejudiced by ignorant and biased
criticisms to go and judge for themselves."[1] That
advice was given about Epstein's first Exhibition at
the 21 Gallery in 1913. To-day much more of his
work is on public exhibition. Some of his earliest
work is to be seen high up on what were once the
British Medical Association's buildings in the Strand
(1908). His other carvings include : the Oscar Wilde
Memorial at Père Lachaise Cemetery, Paris (1912) ;
" Rima," Hyde Park (1925) ; " Day " and " Night,"
on the Underground Building, Broadway, Westminster
(1929) ; and his bronzes are to be found in the Tate
Gallery, the National Gallery, Dublin, the Imperial
War Museum, the Dundee Municipal Gallery, the
Metropolitan Museum, N.Y., Chicago Art Institute,
the Leicester Art Gallery, the Brooklyn Museum, the
Vancouver Art Gallery, the Aberdeen Art Gallery,
the Baltimore Art Institute, the Edinburgh Art Gallery, the Glasgow Art Gallery, the Manchester Art
Gallery, while he has frequent Exhibitions at the
Leicester Galleries in London. I give this long list
of names simply in order that my readers cannot say
what is nearly always said by somebody in a conversation about Epstein : " Well, I have seen photographs
of such and such and I do not like it." A photograph
will give you no idea of a piece of sculpture. Enough

[1] *New Age*, December 25, 1913.

of Epstein's work is publicly exhibited at present to allow almost anyone to visit it and judge for himself. But before he judges, let him have an impartial mind.

I will deal with Epstein's symbolic carvings first of all. I suppose that nearly everyone who goes to see a carving entitled, let us say, " Night," will have a preconceived picture of Night in his mind. If he is the average man and subscribes to *Punch*, he will be influenced by the cartoons of Sir Bernard Partridge and picture Night to himself as a tall woman, not unlike Britannia, in a black cloak, holding in her hands a new lamp-post or some floodlights or whatever happens to be the subject of the cartoon. Or perhaps his idea of Night will be influenced by an illustration in some book he had as a child, and he will expect to see it rendered into sculpture in the form of a relief, showing heavy trees flattened out in a semi-modernistic realistic manner, while five-pointed stars and a moon peep out above them, and quaint little owls, naughty little bats, and wicked little foxes adorn the lower half of the relief. Or perhaps you, reader, are more advanced, and think of Night in abstract terms. In that case I am not going to try to compete with you. But I do not see why you should approach Epstein's carving of " Night " on the Underground Building in London with the ideas of Sir Bernard Partridge, or Edmund Dulac, or Max Ernst already in your mind. When I look at the Nurse Cavell Monument, by the late Sir Reginald Frampton, I do not expect to find in it the qualities that grace a painting by Sir Godfrey Kneller, much as I might welcome the change. Sir Reginald Frampton is as much entitled to his idea of a Nurse Cavell Memorial as anyone else, and certainly the public should not look for qualities in sculpture that are to be found in the utterly different art of painting ; the only objection to the Nurse Cavell Memorial that you can have is that it is not your idea of what such a memorial should be. I will readily admit that it is not mine. But then the late Sir Reginald Frampton was not my idea of an artist. Sir Reginald thought the same about Epstein : " He does not know the A B C of sculpture," he said in a criticism of " Night." Now sweep all this controversy aside, and, if you are in London, go and look at " Night " for yourself. The first thing that will strike you is that the carving subordinates itself to the simplicity of the building. In fact, it looks as though it had been cut out of the building itself, instead of appearing as a messy appendage like the carving on the County Hall, Unilever House, South Africa House, and almost any recent large English building you like to mention. And now for the sculpture itself. A large impersonal being, with a Mongolian face, enormous arms suggesting latent power, is sitting in a composed position with its legs apart. The figure is swathed in heavy drapery, whose few deep-cut folds add to the general strength and impersonal calm of its appearance. Stretched across the knees is the beautifully executed figure of a corpse with arms folded on the breast and legs swinging helplessly out underneath, the foot dangling pathetically inert. The limp weakness of the corpse gives greater strength and majesty to the impersonal being. On the other side of the building, the same impersonal figure is holding up the arms of a little child. That represents " Day." To Epstein Day represents youth and Night death, a reasonable conception, while the impersonal figure, a successful interpretation of the Supreme Being, holds everything in its hands. I would hardly call this work blasphemous. In fact, it seems to me a conception worthy of a poet, executed with consummate skill and paying due regard to its architectural surroundings.

"Night" and "Day," however, are examples of Epstein's carving which will have a more universal appeal than his "Rima." Anyone in his senses can see what they are. With "Rima" the case is more difficult. Rima is the "Bird Goddess" of W. H. Hudson, the writer on natural history, to whom Epstein's sculpture is a memorial in the Bird Sanctuary in Hyde Park. In the first place the carving had to be visible from a path thirty yards away, which ruled out any question of doing a purely illustrative panel in light relief; and in the second place, the area of his design had been predetermined by a committee. Mr. Arnold L. Haskell, in his book *The Sculptor Speaks*,[1] gives us Epstein's opinion of the work. In parenthesis I should say that this book, free from the horrors of art jargon, is the best detailed account of Epstein's work and theories one could hope to read; it is convincing and interesting, being a lively record of Epstein's conversation.

> I was only walking across Hyde Park the other day, and went to see "Rima." I tried to view it as impersonally as possible. The wind was blowing and the leaves falling. It seemed just right. I really cannot understand what all the fuss was about. While I was doing the work in Epping Forest, my wife said, " They will never be able to make a fuss this time." [Smiling.] I shall never forget Mr. Baldwin's expression, though, when he pulled the strings and the work was unveiled.

Later, he goes on to quote the actual passage describing Rima's death, from Hudson's book, which he had in mind when carving the memorial :

> What a distance to fall, through burning leaves and smoke, like a white bird shot dead with a poisoned arrow, swift and straight into that sea of flame below.

[1] Heinemann, 8s. 6d.

Now go and look at " Rima." It is not a bad walk
from the Underground Building. On your way you
will pass that curious mass of contorted marble in
front of Buckingham Palace, the memorial to Queen
Victoria. The smooth academic slickness of the sculpture is much to be expected ; up Constitution Hill you
will see the Quadriga on the top of the arch ; it looks
like an unseemly scuffle going on in a public place.
Then there is the Machine-gun Memorial at Hyde
Park Corner. I have heard this described as " modern
but effective." It represents soldiers, heavily modelled
in bronze, standing with their backs to a block of
Portland stone, bearing a machine gun. After
this slow crescendo to a finale, you come back to
nature with a start as you cross the Park towards
" Rima." Even from a distance, " Rima " among its
trees compels your attention. That is just what a
work of art should do. It should give you a shock,
make you think and feel, and it should dominate the
landscape. For all its domination, Nelson's statue in
Trafalgar Square has never, to my knowledge, been
even discussed as a work of art. And as for the other
statues, except for Charles I and Chantrey's George IV,
I doubt whether one person in a thousand knows what
they look like.

" Rima " is, at least, not undistinguished. Almost
everyone knows what it looks like—that struggling
creature with its arms pressing the sky, sinking between an upward rising eagle and a dove, through the
stone panel down into the earth beneath. The natural
reaction is, " No, I don't like it. It makes me look
at it, but there is something terrible about it." And
then as you continue to look at it, the harmonious design, the play of light and shade, the movement in
" Rima's " body, and the diagonal slope of the composition fix themselves on your mind. And, possibly,

after a time you will realise how much deeper and finer is such a memorial as this, when compared with the little bunny rabbits and fairies of the " Peter Pan " statue in Kensington Gardens. The two works are as different as are Blake and Alfred Noyes, or El Greco and Sir Luke Fildes : the first appeals to your feelings by means of form, the second uses the intercession of associations. To me the first seems the purer and the abler thing to do, and its effect is more lasting on the mind.

Of course, it is likely that " Rima," no matter how one argues, will displease many people just because they have read Hudson, and do not feel as Epstein does about his work. To me " Rima " captures the spirit of Hudson's writing in a marvellous manner. I can think of no other living sculptor who could interpret an author's meaning in stone. I will take a favourite author of mine, Tennyson, and imagine an ambitious sculptural memorial of him by any Royal Academicians. The obvious combination of the May Queen, the Lady of Shalott, and Guinevere standing on a craggy bit of Cornish cliff, comes to the mind, while Sir Lancelot, holding a neat replica of Somersby Rectory, kneels in some bronze rushes below the grass at their feet. Of course this is an exaggeration—though the Cavalry Memorial and the new one to Queen Alexandra, and the R.A.F. Memorial lead one to expect the worst from Academicians—but clearly, the effect conveyed by such a group would not suggest Tennyson, even if one read the inscription underneath. I doubt, too, whether it would arrest the attention, there is so much of that sort of thing about. But wherein lies the true beauty of Tennyson ? His description of landscape, his lyrical qualities, his observation of the minutest forms of nature, and a sense of sky and space engendered in the fens. I do not know how to put that into stone, but I know of only four sculptors in England who would be capable of doing it, and Epstein is one of them.

Thus it is obviously wrong to approach Epstein's " Rima," after what you see of academic effort on the walk from the Underground Building, expecting a literal interpretation of some passage out of Hudson's books. " Yes," you will say, " of course, I don't expect that, but damn it all, when a man is carving a memorial to someone who wrote about nature, he might at least interpret nature accurately instead of *distorting* it."

That's where the public criticism of Epstein always thinks it is in the right. Epstein *distorts* nature. That must be wrong. And that brings us back to the inevitable argument : " Well, if you want an exact replica of nature, have a photograph taken, or if it is sculpture you want, make a plaster cast or a wax model." And somehow that silences further discussion, for by this argument it is impossible even to justify Marcus Stone. Time and again I have heard people say of " Rima " : " It is so distorted ; the hands are too big ; I can see no need for doing that sort of thing." But Epstein, like Michelangelo before him, deliberately accentuates a detail in order to get a desired effect. In the case of " Rima," the large hands complete the balance and rhythm of the design and at the same time give a sense of being in space to the figure, so that it seems only momentarily to be captured in stone, so full of life is it, as it struggles free from the confined area of the panel. And Michelangelo himself, against whom not the most Academic of Academicians will breathe a word, has frequently deliberately accentuated the muscles of his figures in order to give an effect of power. In painting distortion is an accepted necessity. No one has ever claimed that the work, say, of the Italian primitives, El Greco, or the French impressionists has ever successfully portrayed the human figure photographically. Whether in sculpture or in painting, the lines of the human figure, or of anything else, are not to be seen immediately on the surface ; an artist finds new lines for us. That is his function—to give pigment or stone a life of its own conceived in his own brain. It is hard to explain why one shape pleases one man and not another. But it takes an artist to make a pleasing shape. I will borrow from Mr. Haskell again and quote Epstein's account of an amusing occurrence, illustrating this point.

A. L. Haskell. What is art ?

Epstein. I was once asked very much the same question by a judge in a New York Court. A Mr. Steichen had bought Brancusi's well-known abstract work, " The Bird." The United States refused to admit it as a work of art, and charged 40 per cent duty on it as a " manufacture of metal." Steichen protested, and I was called in as an expert witness. This is what happened, after a long inquiry as to my qualifications :

District Attorney. Are you prepared to call this a bird ?

Epstein. If the sculptor calls it a bird, I am quite satisfied.

Judge. If you saw it in the forest, would you shoot it ?

Epstein. That is not the only way to identify a bird.

Judge. Why is this a work of art ?

Epstein. Because it satisfies my sense of beauty. I find it a beautiful object.

Judge. So a highly polished, harmoniously curved brass rail could also be a work of art ?

Epstein. Yes, it could become so.

Customs Officer. Then a mechanic could have done this thing ?

Epstein. No, he could have polished it, but he could never have conceived it.

We finally won the case.

A. L. Haskell. Then you could not give a more comprehensive definition of art ?

Epstein. No, not one that would be of the slightest use. All I can say is what I told the judge, my own personal reaction : " This is a work of art because it satisfies my sense of beauty." No one can say much more.

This incident helps, more than any theorising, to an interpretation of Epstein's carvings. The best thing to do is to approach his work without prejudices and previous mental pictures of what it ought to look like. No one liking poetry, and reading Shelley's " Moon " for the first time, would think of saying, " He *ought* to have written this or that, as Wordsworth or Shenstone would have done." Why, therefore, *ought* Epstein to acquire the mind of Watts, Leighton, Frampton, Reynold-Stephens, Chantrey or Jagger ? If English people had the perception of the visual arts that they have of literature, there would be more hope for English sculpture.

Poor Epstein, his trouble is that he is a three-dimensional artist in a country which judges by two-dimensional standards. This is only a recent development. The grand age which made Westminster Abbey a repository of the works of such men of genius as Roubiliac, Flaxman, Wilton, Rysnack, Nollekens, the Bacons, Smith and Chantrey, is not far removed from the present generation of arty deans and chapters who want to clear their works away. Yes, the very deans and chapters who want to remove such statues and decorate the empty spaces with Pre-Raphaelite hangings come from that generation which has let every decent English churchyard be filled with glaring Italian marble crosses, sentimental angels, and Aberdeen granite obelisks, and has stuck the walls of village churches with tawdry brasses and vulgar or " refeened " memorials— a generation bred on romantic literature, grounded in the Royal Academy, and finally plunging into a Celtic twilight, never to emerge. Salutary as were the sour grapes in other respects, the children's teeth are set on edge. One thing at least the romantic generation has acquired, and that is, a blind veneration for the past. Many deans and many chapters would give the æsthetic and unbiased consideration to some piece of grotesque carving in one of their cathedral churches that they would not think of giving to Epstein. Yet their Gothic carvings of evil spirits or good, as gargoyles or in bench-ends, rood-screens and misereres, are surely as much and more a distortion of nature than the public carvings of Epstein ? Let me press home the argument in favour of *life* in sculpture as opposed to mere photography, by one more instance.

From my earliest childhood I have owned an old Teddy Bear called Archibald. His head is the shape of a large inverted pear ; his eyes are brown wool with white wool in the middle ; his body is egg-shaped, and he has tubular arms much longer than his legs. His paws are padded with some sort of cambric, and his expression is that of one who contemplates infinity from very near to. So deeply written upon my mind is the shape and expression of old Archibald, that when the word " bear " occurs in conversation and someone is talking, perhaps about Polar Bears in Greenland, I think of lots of animals looking like Archie, rolling about on the Polar ice. Yet I went to the Dublin Zoo the other day and saw a Polar Bear at close quarters. It bore no resemblance to Archie at all. The eyes were small and wicked, the head was diminutive and cunning, and only in the shape of the body was there a suggestion that Archie came from the same species. Yet there is no denying that while being so different from a Polar Bear, Archie is undoubtedly a bear, although in detail he differs from all bears.

Archie is to me a work of art as much as was Brancusi's Bird to Epstein. He satisfies my sense of beauty, as once he comforted my childish sorrow. I chose such a homely example of the sculptor's art—Archie, by the way, was made in a toy factory—because it is when he is at the stage of liking dolls and bears and other stuffed animals that the average Englishman is nearest appreciating sculpture. Thereafter the literary quality, that I have mentioned, comes into his appreciation, and it may be said, without reserve, that stuffed animals and dolls are the only examples of pure form appreciated for its own sake in England. It takes a lot of sophistication and conscious effort to shift the burden of literary association and meet pure form face to face again.

I have hitherto dealt entirely with Epstein's carvings —that is to say, his work in stone—largely because it is more for the public eye, metaphorically and otherwise, than is his work in bronze, and also because it is so stupidly ridiculed. When Sir Reginald Blomfield, the late Sir Reginald Frampton, and the late Sir Frank Dicksee have said a thing is bad, you may be sure it is good. These three and a postman and a policeman (reported in the *Evening Standard*) started a newspaper outburst about " Night " and " Day," to which I have already alluded. They were opposed, however, by Mr. H. G. Wells, Mr. Bernard Shaw, Mr. C. F. A. Voysey, Sir William Orpen, Sir James Barrie, Edgar Wallace, Wilenski, and many others, including Mr. Hugh Walpole, who wrote in a letter to the *Manchester Guardian* : " It is difficult to judge Mr. Epstein's sculptured figures from photographs, but even in the photographs they are extremely interesting. Taking the photographs in conjunction with the names and expressed views of those who condemn Mr. Epstein's work, I should suppose the figures to be masterpieces."

7

But it is no use my continuing a sermon on how to look at Epstein's carving. If you like the shapes he carves, after you have received the first shock at seeing something you don't expect, then Epstein will have justified himself. But do not say he is incompetent or echo the sentiment of the late Sir Reginald Frampton, that he does not know the A B C of sculpture. He is a most accomplished craftsman, and his bronzes, which anyone can appreciate, since they are " like " the people they represent, will dispel any public impression that he is incompetent.

His bronzes I have left to the last. There are more of them, as it seems to be his favourite material, but they speak for themselves, since they are, in almost all cases, portraits. But whereas a portrait in oils shows only one aspect of a figure from a certain angle, a bust has to be a portrait from countless angles, and no photograph can do it justice. Epstein works in the same bold poetical way over an intricate piece of portraiture as he does over a piece of monumental carving. He avoids any effect of mathematical correctness, which we can see in most Edwardian and late Victorian sculpture dotted about our towns. Such sculpture hardly ranks as portraiture, and the sublime insipidity into which the faces have been changed of these once famous people makes it impossible to-day to distinguish between General Havelock or General Napier, Councillor Robinson or Alderman Cleeves. Epstein realises that the two sides of a face are never alike, and he exaggerates this dissimilarity. His bust of Ramsay MacDonald is a particular instance ; one eye is a fraction lower than the other, so is the brow, and the horizontal cleft in the chin is not quite parallel with the lips. It is not until one has looked at the bust for some time that these details become apparent. Then, when they have all been absorbed, the portrait is not merely a likeness—but a speaking likeness.

Probably no artist, save Rembrandt, has been such a master of light as Epstein. By means of the rough texture of his portrait busts, he is able to create shadows and heights in the face so that the bronze becomes flesh. It is possible to see this rough texture imitated by more prolific sculptors, and it at once becomes apparent that they do not know what they are at. They make the features jagged in an uncomprehending effort to be " modern." The subtle exaggeration of a remarkable feature in a face and the use of texture to convey light are never better displayed than where Epstein is modelling a bust from someone of his own choice. For this reason the busts of Iris Tree and of his daughter Peggy Jean are, for me, the most satisfying.

Epstein's bronzes speak for themselves. For the unprejudiced, so do his carvings. But when Epstein creates a work of art he does not want it to be judged by the reader of *Punch* whose taste has long ago been weaned to the gentle academics of Academicians, nor by the newspaper reporter out for a scoop, nor by the Bloomsbury monarch seeking the abstract and ever escaping it. He creates a work of art to please himself, just as any other artist does. And that brings us back to the beginning of the dissertation—what is Epstein, after all, when he has been exonerated from blasphemy, worshipping ugliness, lack of patriotism, etc., etc.? He is a Jew, and like all Jews subject to influences. During his career he has run the whole gamut of sculpture, admiring and being helped by, but never copying, styles so varied as the Egyptian, Japanese, Negroid, and the abstract Greek. The sculpture that appeals to him most is, I believe, the African, and it seems to have appealed to him for a long time.

Mr. Haskell quotes him as saying that negro sculpture
is governed by the same considerations that govern
all sculpture.

> In every good school of sculpture there are certain values
> quite apart from any interest in the object represented. The
> *Venus de Milo* is very much more than just a beautiful woman.
> The person who will not look or feel beyond the representa-
> tion itself, cannot comprehend the very essence of sculpture,
> though he will persuade himself that he understands the
> Greek ideal, and that the work of the primitive negro is
> unworthy of study.

And what Epstein appreciates in Negro sculpture is
its blending of abstract forms—that is to say, pleasing
shapes—with an underlying naturalism, a likeness to
the human figure. It suggests new ways, outside the
inevitable classical one, of interpreting nature.

Epstein is not primitive nor is he " modern." He
is an artist who, by some freak of chance, has gained a
reputation in a country which has somewhat stereo-
typed sculptural conventions. The " moderns " are
those who are typical of their generation's theories of
what sculpture should be. Epstein is too important
to belong to any period at all.

SIGMUND FREUD
By Philip Lindsay

SIGMUND FREUD

SIGMUND FREUD[1]

By Philip Lindsay

As a boy, Sigmund Freud dreamed continually of going to Rome. This seems a queer dream for a Jewish lad to have, but much is explained when we learn that in his mind Judaism was associated with Hannibal. In attempting to estimate Freud we must not forget this fact—the fact that he was a Jew and that he dreamed of a Judaic Hannibal. Not that he wished consciously to destroy anything, far from it ; he wished to create, but he also wished to conquer, and that he succeeded even his most violent enemies must confess. Much of his work has yet to be sifted ; he says himself that he does not know what verdict the future will pronounce on psycho-analysis ; that does not concern us here. What we can state definitely is that the effect of his discoveries has been almost incalculable. Like all great efforts, religious or scientific, his work brought with it both good and bad, it was hated beyond its dangers and estimated beyond its value. But its effect was enormous, and for this reason alone—no matter whether one reverences or detests psycho-analysis—one must not under-estimate

---

[1] Unless otherwise stated, the quotations in this essay are from Freud's own works, particularly his *Selbstdarstellung*, printed in the *Gesammelte Schriften*, and published by the Internationaler Psychoanalytischer Verlag (1928), and from *Die Widerstände gegen die Psychoanalyse*, first printed in *La Revue Juive*, 1920. I have also used *The Interpretation of Dreams*, trans. by A. A. Brill ; *The Psychopathology of Everyday Life*, trans. by A. A. Brill, and Fritz Wittells's *Sigmund Freud : His Personality, His Teaching, and His School*, trans. by Eden and Cedar Paul (1924). For permission to quote from these translations I must thank Messrs. Allen & Unwin, who possess the copyright. I would also like to thank Mr. Philip Owens for his great help, and particularly Dr. Ernest Jones, the President of the International Psycho-Analytical Association, for his kindness in looking through the proofs, although all responsibility for any statement in this essay is wholly mine.

it. The first rush of excitement has ebbed, and at last psycho-analysis can find its place as a purely clinical affair, as a dangerous science not to be meddled with by laymen.

Psycho-analysis was begun by a Jew, and Freud himself considers this a significant fact. I feel that only a Jew could have fully unearthed its treasures, its beauties and its horrors ; only a Jew could have realised those hidden springs of the mind, only a Jew could have battled so magnificently for them when found.

On Freud's wall hangs a reproduction of Ingres' Œdipus questioning the Sphinx ; a sketch of this painting is stamped upon the title-pages of the official psychoanalytic publications, and this mother-son, father-daughter complex—the legacy of Œdipus who murdered his father and married his mother—is the great thesis that dominates all Freud's work ; it is perhaps the most profound truth that psycho-analysis has yet given us. I doubt if any other religion could have made a man realise such a thought. Christianity is too idealised, it hides men from even the memoried torture of the Cross, by stressing faith, love, and charity, but the Judaic religion still maintains, in all its majesty and terror, the worship of a jealous god, of a father of lightning and plagues. It is a patriarchal religion, curiously awful to the uninitiated, and most binding to its devotees. Here the son is not worshipped as Christians worship him ; Jews do not pray to a pitiful god-man who died for love of his brothers, but to a father august and remorseless.

From this faith sprang the knowledge of psycho-analysis, the knowledge of the father-mother worship, the answer to the sphinx's riddle. Who but a Jew could have realised this so forcibly ? Who but a Jew, with centuries of massacre behind him, could have appreciated the subtle tortures of the mind, the sweet delight of sadism, the ecstatic agonies of masochism ? The tortures of a race must become translated into pleasure if the race is to endure, and the desire for retaliation, pushed back into the unconscious, must become sadistic. The years of burning flesh and broken bodies have taught the Jew a deep and frightful knowledge of man at his basest and at his noblest, man the tortured, the maimed and suffering creature, and man the glorious triumphant martyr. Truly I cannot see how any other race could have learned and appreciated so fully the deepest impulses in man.

And Freud comes from a family that has suffered. He tells us, in his *Psychopathology of Everyday Life*, how, when travelling to England to meet his half-brother, he almost missed his train at Cologne. At first he could not understand why this should have happened, but now he realises that it was because of

a feeling of piety, for according to an old family tradition, my ancestors were once expelled from this city during a persecution of the Jews.

And again, in his *Selbstdarstellung*, he is reminded of this ancient pogrom. It was not forgotten, it became one of the heritages of the family. And during his own life in Vienna he suffered from a more subtle pogrom, from the contempt and hatred of his fellow-students at the university. He was a Jew, an outcast, despised, and this attitude drove him violently into his studies. He determined to prove that a Jew can be as great as the men about him ; and he proved it, to the whole world he proved it.

Driven inwards by this sense of inferiority (and of superiority), the Jew must turn always to himself, he must build his own world, must find comfort therein, and courage and heroism. From this inward world,

this world of dreamed-of glories and of the memory
of ghastly tortures, psycho-analysis was born. It is
almost, one might say, a different Judaism, containing
the most profound truths.

Let us examine briefly the main outline of Freud's
life. For these facts we must rely almost wholly on
his own works, particularly on the all-too-brief *Selbstdarstellung* (to my knowledge not yet translated into
English, most unfortunately), on *The Interpretation
of Dreams*, and the *Psychopathology of Everyday Life*.
All through his books are scattered personal anecdotes,
and of course numerous tales are repeated of him, as
they are of all great men. These verbal tales I have
completely ignored in this essay, and I have relied
almost entirely on his own works and, very slightly, on
the rather scandalous *Sigmund Freud : His Personality,
His Teaching and His School*, by Fritz Wittels, who
has, however, since publicly retracted the distorted
presentation the book gave.

Freud was born at Freiburg, Moravia (now Czechoslovakia), on May 6, 1856. " My parents," he tells us,
" were Jews, and I am still a Jew." From the age of
four he lived in Vienna, and at school he showed a
prodigious memory almost worthy of Dean Swift.
Although his parents were very poor, they wished
him to follow his own desires, and his father insisted
that he choose his studies himself. But that was not
easy to do. His one desire was the desire for knowledge, he wished to be a sort of Goethe, a literary
man, a scientist, and a philosopher ; he lusted after
knowledge in all its forms, knowledge " more, however,
in relation to human rather than to scientific objects."
It was Darwin who inspired him, Darwin and Goethe.
In fact, it was after hearing a lecture on Goethe's *Die
Natur* that he definitely decided to take up medicine,
but he found little enthusiasm for it. As yet, nothing

seemed to attract him deeply, for all roads to knowledge were equally splendid, equally enticing. He travelled the road of medicine, but he glanced over his shoulder at those other roads, regretfully, unsure if he had chosen rightly.

The university classes must have been torture to such a sensitive mind. He suffered strongly there, " principally," he remarks, " because I found myself inferior, unable to mix with people, being a Jew." That was the general atmosphere of the university, and greatly as we must be revolted by it we should also offer it a vote of thanks. Who knows that perhaps if young Freud had mixed freely with the others his energies might have become dissipated ? He might never have discovered the great truths that he was fated to discover if he had not been forced into loneliness and hurt pride. The contemptuous hatred around must have stiffened him, must have driven him deeper into his studies, however tiresome they seemed. We all know the desire to rise above our fellows, but if those fellows should go out of their way to jeer at us, how much greater would be that desire ! There is a story about the young Balzac falling over during a dance ; when the minxes laughed at him, he swore that he would " show them," which he did. Naturally genius cannot be reduced to simple terms like this, but there must be a great deal of the inferiority complex in all geniuses. Half the lust for achievement is the lust to prove to one's friends (and to oneself) that the man they laugh at is greater than they dream of.

I have never understood why I should be ashamed of my origin [writes Freud in the *Selbstdarstellung*], or why anyone should speak to me of racial questions. I was content to be an alien . . . In my opinion, there was room for an honest worker inside humanity.

And this he has proved splendidly ; automatically he rejected the antagonism about him, it made him " independent."

It was not really until Freud went to Paris in 1885 to work under Charcot that he saw the twinkle ahead that was later to flare into psycho-analysis. He was very poor at this time, and for hours he would sit on top of Notre Dame, dreaming over the beautiful city spread beneath his feet, the city that was there for him to conquer—a Jewish Hannibal looking from the alps towards the Christian world. And he worked hard, driven by poverty and his aspirations. Already he saw a glimpse of the road ahead. A family friend, Dr. Josef Breuer, had revealed to him a most amazing fact : symptoms of hysteria had been cured in a patient in a special way during hypnosis ; when hypnotised the patient had revealed the origin of the hysteria and its emotions, and had been thereby cured. Freud did not forget this, and under the influence of Charcot he found courage to face the problems of which he was as yet but half aware. He used hypnotism, but later discarded it ; cures were never permanent when made that way ; he was searching for subtler methods, for psychological methods. He was already a Docent in Neuro-pathology, yet his ideas were scoffed at by his colleagues ; with the patience of tired " great men " they pointed out that hysteria cannot possibly refer to males when the actual word is built upon a feminine basis. Later, on his deathbed, one of these men—one of these men who so derided Freud's efforts—was to confess shamefully that he had always been a male hysteric ! Freud did not give in, he continued quietly at his researches, now and then publishing important works on neurology, particularly on aphasia and on children's cerebral paralyses.

It was with Breuer, however, that he took the really

gigantic step, with Breuer who had first revealed to him the path. With him he collaborated in a book called *Studien über Hysterie* (1895) and from then on there was no faltering. Breuer had not really wished to publish this work, but his young friend's enthusiasm drove him forward ; immediately after, the collaborators were to part, but that was after Freud first stated his theory of sex, of the gigantic importance of sex in the unconscious life. Probably glad to escape, Breuer hurried back to his work on organic diseases ; again, the path was a lonely one for Freud, but he did not flinch from it.

He was hated, his great researches were reviled. Now he had finally discarded hypnotism and worked on the free association method, on what was to become the psycho-analytic method. After his separation from Breuer he was for ten years utterly alone. Those ten years of isolation would have defeated a lesser spirit than his ; perhaps it was the Jew in him that made him keep on so fearlessly. This was no new experience, he had been shunned at the universities and attacked in Paris ; the Jew does not fear isolation, for in that can be found self-respect.

From 1906 on, the hatred lessened, and slowly the followers came. His work began to sift into the world, to be loved by a few, misunderstood by most, and hated by many.

The outline of such a life as Freud's must necessarily be brief when written by a layman for laymen. It is really with reluctance that I do not quote from the many fascinating details of his medical career given in the *Selbstdarstellung*. But it would be of little use for me in this essay to detail his gradual discoveries, the extraordinary patience and courage with which he continued alone, and with which he listened to the jeers and the cruel insults. Besides, the history of the psycho-analytical movement has been written too often to be repeated here, where I must be brief. Freud writes in the *Selbstdarstellung* :

> Finally, the author in all modesty must ask this question— whether his own personality as a Jew, as one who has never attempted to hide his Jewishness, has not played a great part in the world antipathy [to psycho-analysis] ? Although this has never been openly stated, he has unfortunately become suspicious enough to believe that this antipathy has not been without its effect. It is perhaps also no mere chance that the first psycho-analyst was a Jew. In order to acknowledge this it required considerable courage to face a destiny of loneliness against opposition, a destiny more natural to the Jew than to anyone else.

And as he remarks in another work, " He who knows how to wait need make no concessions."

I have often wondered why, in the innumerable essays on psycho-analysis, Freud's Jewish side has not —to my knowledge—been more strongly stressed. Perhaps by stressing it the average writer is afraid that he will thereby reveal much of the reason for his hatred of psycho-analysis, for it is the work of a Jew. And as I have already remarked, I doubt if anybody but a Jew could have made such profound discoveries.

To the shame of every Gentile it must be confessed that Freud is not overstating the truth in the above passage. The hatred of psycho-analysis was terrific at first, it was almost insane. It still does exist here and there, although in a much lesser form. It was Freud's refusal to compromise that most outraged the critics. He knew how to wait. He remarks that, if instead of the word " love " he had used " eros," half the hatred would have disappeared ; words mean so much to the human race. Women can conquer their modesty by lisping in baby-fashion about things that were a few years ago unmentionable. Undies, teddies, nighties, step-ins, knickers, are safe words ;

they have no ugly or passionate associations. By using a phraseology of this type, by coining grotesque words from the Greek or Latin, Freud could have avoided much of the hatred he aroused. But he knew that once one step is given in, it is not long before all the defences crumble. A fighter must not lose his nerve, he must be outright, straightforward. When a young airman crashes his instructor sends him up again immediately ; he must restore his confidence. It is much the same in other things ; if a man surrenders to one fear, it is not long before all sorts of fears swoop upon him, destroy him. But Freud was a Jew, and he had the stubborn arrogance of a Jew. With an heroic disregard for people's feelings, he stressed every essential of psycho-analysis ; and with almost hysterical hatred the people rejected it. As Stephan Zweig remarks in his illuminating work, *Die Heilung durch den Geist*, it was Freud's task

> to reveal humanity to itself—to reveal it, but not to make it happier.

And humanity's one desire is to be made happier, to be made peaceful ; in other words, to cling to its repressions. I fully agree with Freud that many repressions are healthy, are actually essential, but that does not detract from the truth that many of them are most dangerous, not only to individuals, but to humanity at large.

It is easy therefore to understand the reaction of hatred that exploded on Freud ; man did not want to know himself if thereby he would be made unhappy. Yet beyond this, I feel there was also the hatred for the Jew. If Freud had been a Gentile he would have been attacked, as Lister, Pasteur, Galileo and Darwin were attacked, but I doubt if he would have been attacked quite so venomously as he was.

Freud himself is not Judaic and never was, yet he
is very serious on the question of nationalism,
particularly for the Jew, for nationalism is only an
imitation of father-worship. Thŭrefore he is a member of the Jewish freemason's lodge, Bene Brith.
The Jew must build a world within a world, his
people alone can give him courage, belief in his
people will let him face insults and rebuffs without
shame.

We have had proved to us in recent times the German
attitude to the Jew ; the Nazis are merely a culmination of this hatred ; they are not a sudden rootless
expression of it. At the age of ten or twelve Freud
was told by his father that when he was a lad he was
walking one Saturday afternoon along the village street.
He was very well dressed, and was wearing a fine new
fur cap. Then a Christian happened to pass ; he
noted the fine new fur cap and he went up and knocked
the cap into the mud, shouting, " Jew ! get off the
pavement ! " When told this story, little Freud gazed
up wonderingly at his adored father. " What did you
do ? " he asked. " I went into the street," replied
his father, " and I picked up the cap."

From then onwards, Hannibal, not papa, became
Freud's hero ; he reverenced above all men that fierce
Carthaginian soldier who, when but a boy, swore
undying hatred of Rome and who almost destroyed
Rome. Rome was obviously the symbol for Christianity, and Hannibal meant the Jewish conqueror. It
was in such fantasies as this that the boy kept whole
the integrity of his spirit against the inexplicable hatred
of those around him. He had also another hero. On
the backs of his wooden soldiers he pasted the names of
famous soldiers. And his most beloved amongst them
was Masséna (Jew, Menasse), Napoleon's *enfant gâté de
la victoire*, for a time commander of the army of Rome.

From childhood, then, Freud was forced to realise his nationalism ; he had to be told by a calm father that that magnificent father—the god—had once had his cap knocked off into the mud by a lout of a Christian. A terrible thought for any boy to face ! No wonder Hannibal became his hero, Hannibal the soldier, the leader, the enemy of Rome ! The Jew must have his nationalism, without that he is lost ; it is his armour, the one buckler he can hold against an enemy world. One of the usual attacks on the Jews is that they refuse to mix with other nations, that they refuse to be absorbed ; but they dare not try the experiment, it is too dangerous. They might lose their ego, their world, in the process. And nationalism is actually father-worship, particularly in Germany and Austria. (England is more sentimental, it has a motherland, not a fatherland ; this can sometimes be even more dangerous an attitude, as witness the Irish with their astounding and often murderous adoration of Mother Erin.) But mother or father worship, that does not matter ; either way it is the child's love for the parent, the Œdipus complex, that most gigantic of all psychoanalytic facts. And the Jews are undoubtedly even more nationalistic than Germans, Irishmen, or Corsicans. From both inward and outward ideals—both the Jewish and the Austrian—Freud learned the vital truth on which life is based, the fixation of the child's absorbent libido towards one of its parents.

We can appreciate the tormented life he must have lived in Vienna and Paris by the surprise with which he speaks of the United States of America. He could not believe his ears and eyes when he went there—although the food, it is said, permanently ruined his digestion—for in this queer country he was actually treated as a Christian ! Nobody shunned him, nobody knocked his hat into the mud or spat when he passed ; and he

gazed about him with childlike amazement and joy.
That to me is more tragic even than the awful insults
he suffered at home. It is a terrible thought that a
man of Freud's extraordinary intellect, one of the
world figures for all time, should be touched and made
happy by a few kind words !

> In Europe [he tells us in the *Selbstdarstellung*] I felt like
> an outlaw, but here I found myself looked upon as an equal
> by the finest people !

The finest people ! How few of them could have
reached a quarter-way to Freud's mental height !
And again, " It was like realising a daydream ! "
Without doubt Freud had been tortured. No man
could have suffered what he has suffered without being
tortured. And it is tragic and rather pathetic to find
that he speaks quite bitterly about many of his old
colleagues and disciples. He has lost three of the
oldest, Jung, Stekel, and Adler. The quarrel with
Adler and Jung was evidently on purely scientific
matters, but the quarrel with Stekel still appears to
be a mystery. As Wittels remarks, Freud speaks of
Stekel as if he " had been caught pocketing the
spoons ! " It is useless for us to speculate about these
quarrels, they are personal matters which should be
left alone ; but every facet of Freud's character is to
me important, so greatly do I reverence the man and
his work, and I feel that some passing mention should
be made here to what Wittels makes so inordinately
important. That Freud is hurt by these quarrels he
himself tells us, and he speaks of Jung and Adler as
" heretics." Perhaps they are heretics, but often a
schism can throw light on the truth. No one can
doubt the value of Jung's work, nor, in a lesser degree,
of Adler's. Stekel's work on frigidity and impotence
has been of great importance. Yet great as these men

are, we must never forget that Freud gave them the magic key. It is the inevitable result of all scientific work that the pioneers must be superseded ; yet after all, theirs is the greatest work. Jung, Stekel, and Adler may have explored branches of psychoanalysis, the main stream still bears the name of Freud, and it always will bear it, no matter how important the branches may become.

Much could be—and has been—made of these personal affairs, particularly as Freud himself remarks, in his *Psychopathology of Everyday Life*, that

> I am usually rather resentful and cannot forget a single incident of an episode that has annoyed me.

All great men must suffer the pain of having their private lives ravished by literary dung-beetles, and Freud has left himself sadly open to attack ; courageously he has given us his dreams, his most secret thoughts, his petty quarrels with his wife, his dream-efforts to degrade his father—all the small details that we strive to hide, the little things of which we are more ashamed than we are of the really bad acts we have committed. Freud unashamedly brings almost everything forth for us to examine, perhaps because he has so little to hide, for it is significant that none of his detractors has attempted really to blacken his character. And a man who stresses sex in his work leaves himself peculiarly open to be traduced. The average man, with a dirty private life, is always eager to bellow at expressions of frankness ; he does it, like an octopus with ink, to hide his own sins. Personally, I suspect a man who denounces wickedness far more swiftly than I do one who attempts to glorify it. The Beardsleys of life are often sadly moral. And, no matter what the average repressed animal might think, a man like Freud has nothing whatever to conceal. He can afford to be frank, he can afford to face the unimportant yet unpleasant facts which he reveals so unblushingly, because he knows the integrity of his own spirit, the cleanliness of his own mind.

Forgive this wandering digression, but I do not think it can be stated sufficiently that a philosophy should not be related to a man's actions. Nietzsche preached freedom, but himself was as holy as a monk. And Nietzsche, I have been told, is one of Freud's favourite philosophers ; Nietzsche and Schopenhauer seem to be his particular loves. Wittels remarks that nowadays, when he slips off for a holiday, an edition of Schopenhauer usually bulges out of his pocket.

As a worker Freud is evidently amazing, and he has no secretary; everything he writes is written by hand. For forty years or so he had handled eight, nine, ten or eleven cases a day. He works from nine in the morning until eight at night, and at night he starts writing and usually does not finish until about 1 a.m. He sleeps thoroughly, undisturbed, for seven hours. On Saturday he gives himself a holiday: he plays cards. Until he reached the age of seventy he never suffered a second's illness. For over seventy years he has lived in the one town, for over forty years in the one house.

. . . I wonder if these stray facts reveal the man. To see Freud clearly, and to revere and love him, I feel that one must turn to his own books. It is impossible to over-estimate his discoveries. Before he began work, all neuroses were explained by heredity or by degeneration ; Freud proved the power of the mind over the body, and his really superb discovery was the realisation that sex-life began, not at puberty, but at birth itself.

I cannot detail the great achievements he has reached, and no detailing could give the least idea of their magnitude. Their effect on life is proof enough of their importance and of their validity. Even people who do not know his name have been affected by his teachings. Truly, Hannibal has looked at last on Rome !

Whatever your attitude may be towards psychoanalysis, you cannot help but respect Freud, you cannot help respecting his courage and his amazing patience and his quiet contempt of attacks. In other words, you cannot help respecting the particularly Jewish qualities in him—although, of course, I do not mean to say that these qualities are not often shared by other nations. Yet only a Jew could have faced what Freud faced ; and despite the magnificent defiance, one sees, under the brave show, a certain shrinking.

He is defiant, perhaps, because he suffers so deeply, because he is so conscious of his race and of the hatred about him. It is not pleasant to live amidst hatred. The Jew has been trained to withstand it ; for centuries he has steeled his heart with patience and masked his face with scornful disregard, yet under the armour there must be fear and, perhaps, a certain bewilderment. Wittels remarks how Freud likes to have with him sympathetic listeners, but that is a failing common to most of us—if failing it can be called ; even if they are not particularly intelligent their interest delights him, it salves his egoism, bruised for so long by ridicule, and worse.

Freud has fought for so long, it is time that he was given peace and understanding. From the very beginning, at the Vienna University, he had to face contempt ; in Paris, too, he was lonely, fighting slowly forward without real encouragement. He gives much of the credit for the discovery of psycho-analysis to Breuer, yet Breuer never realised that neuroses had anything beyond a physiological basis. It rested with Freud to prove—working on the discoveries of others,

like Breuer, Charcot and Chrobak, the gynæcologist—
that neuroses were mental and could be cured only by
special treatment. The theory of repression was his,
although it has been said (quite untruthfully) that he
based the idea on Schopenhauer's suggestions. When
he started in Vienna as a doctor he was utterly ignorant
of his real work and of the truth about neuroses. It
was no sudden discovery, it was a gradual process of
thought, of linking each new case to another case. This
period of loneliness he himself calls a " beautiful and
heroic time." Most certainly it was that, but it must
also have been a terrible time. To anybody other than
a Jew it would have been practically unbearable.

What does Freud look like personally ? We have
many photographs of him, and all are alike, with
prominent nose, strong eyes, and hard, white, pointed
beard. I have never met him, but may I quote from
one who has, Fritz Wittels ?

> His black hair, slightly grizzled, was smooth and was
> parted on the left side. His beard was small, and was
> trimmed to a point. Many celebrities have large and
> piercing eyes, but Freud is an exception. Freud's eyes are
> dark brown and lustrous ; they have a scrutinising ex-
> pression as they look up at one. He is slender, of medium
> height, brisk in his movements ; but his figure was slightly
> bowed when I first knew him. He had the student's stoop.

Detailed as that description is, we do not see the
man ; no photograph, no written picture, can show
him to us. We must turn to his books, to those amazing books that are scholarly, philosophic, scientific, and
autobiographical. He writes with a clear, straightforward style ; there is no confusion of ideas, no muddling
of terms. Here we can indeed see the man, we can
see his patience, his courage, and his good humour.
Yes, there is good humour too in his writings. It

has been said that many of the jokes quoted in his *Wit
and the Unconscious* are quite pointless ; they are to
Gentiles, for most of them here—and in *The Psychopathology of Everyday Life*—are distinctly Jewish, and
those Jews to whom I have told them, thought them
extraordinarily funny. That is why this book, to
Christian readers like myself, sits lowest in the shelf—
probably next to *Totem and Taboo*.

We cannot disentangle the Jew from most of Freud's
work. He has never attempted to do so himself.
From the boy dreaming of Hannibal to the conqueror
of the mind, Freud is essentially Jewish. We should
feel grateful for that. It was the Jew who conquered
because only a Jew would have had the courage to
conquer and to face the bitterest attacks. A Christian
would probably have surrendered, or would at least
have compromised—and to compromise is fatal. The
enemy can only be defeated by silence. That was how
Freud conquered.

LUIGI LUZZATTI
By Luigi Villari

Luigi Luzzatti

LUIGI LUZZATTI

By Luigi Villari

FEW countries have been so free from anti-Semitism as Italy. Under the old pre-Risorgimento Governments Jews were subject to certain disabilities, and they had been expelled from the Neapolitan Kingdom when it was part of the Spanish dominions. In all other parts of Italy they were free to settle, even if they were obliged to live in Ghettoes. In Venice, in Tuscany, and in the Papal States they were treated relatively with favour—for some centuries the Pope's *archiatra* or physician-in-ordinary was by tradition a Jew. By the nineteenth century the legal and political disabilities had been almost wholly eliminated, and with the establishment of the Italian Kingdom they were entirely swept away. The Constitution of the Kingdom of Sardinia of 1848 had already removed them from the statute-book as far as concerned its own territories, and in the next two decades that instrument was extended to the rest of the peninsula.

Even social discrimination against the Jews, which outlasted the legal disabilities, soon disappeared, although traces of it survived here and there. Jews have for long been placed on a footing of equality with Christians in all fields of activity, including the army, the navy, the civil services and the professions, admitted to the best society, except in a few old-fashioned circles, and not a few have had titles of nobility conferred on them. In politics it was no handicap to be a Jew. Italy has had one Jewish Prime Minister—the subject of this essay—and another, Sidney Sonnino, who, although a Christian by religion, was the son of a Jewish father (incidentally he proved one of the ablest,

most patriotic, and honest statesmen the country ever
had). Many other Jews have held Ministerial rank ;
one, General Ottolenghi, was Minister of War, and to-
day, in the Fascist Government, the Minister of Finance, Guido Jung, is of Jewish origin, while many
other Jews hold high positions in the public service.

The reasons for the absence of anti-Semitism in
Italy are principally two—the small number of Jews
residing in the country, and the character of Italian
Jews. Out of a total population of 42,000,000, only
one per thousand are Jews. The immense majority of
them are of the Sephardim branch exiled from Spain
at the time of the *Reyes católicos*, or later immigrants
from the Levant who were themselves of Spanish
origin. Very few of the Italian Jews are poor, and
there are not those seething masses of Jewish prole-
tarians which elsewhere cause so much trouble of a
social and economic nature. Above all, the Italian
Jews have for the most part been resident in the country
for many generations, and even if they retain their old
religion—to which indeed many of them are deeply
attached—they have been completely absorbed into
the body of the nation and regard themselves and are
regarded by their neighbours as thorough Italians.
Jews played an honourable part in the Risorgimento,
and the numbers of Jews who fought and died for their
country in the World War are considerable, as may be
seen from the rolls of honour in the various synagogues.

There are, even in Italy, certain people who are
prejudiced against Jews, just as there are some North
Italians who are prejudiced against Southerners or
Sicilians, and there are a few clubs to which Jews
are not easily admitted. But nowhere is there any
mass feeling against the Jews as such. There was a
moment after the outbreak of the Russian Revolution,
many of whose leaders in the early days of Bolshevism

were Jews, when certain expressions of anti-Semitism occurred in Italy as in every other country on both sides of the Atlantic. But they did not last; very few of the Italian subversive leaders were Jews, and in fact the immense majority of Italian Jews had no sympathy of any kind with Bolshevism or Communism. To-day it is safe to say that anti-Semitism is non-existent in Italy.

Venetia is one of the regions where Jews have always been most numerous and where they early attained positions of prominence in all walks of life. One of the leading Jewish families in the city of Venice a hundred years ago was that of the Luzzatti. It had been settled there for four centuries, having come, according to family tradition, from Silesia, whence the Jews had been at that time expelled. As evidence of the consideration which the family enjoyed, its members had been granted the right by the Republic to wear black hats instead of red or yellow ones. It lived, when the subject of this essay was born, in the Palazzo Michiel, an old patrician house on the Fondamenta delle Sense in the Sestiere di Cannareggio,[1] outside the old Ghetto, but near it. Marco, the father of Luigi Luzzatti, was a well-to-do wholesale dealer in wool, hemp, and rice, and the owner of two small woollen mills. As was the custom of most of the old Venetian Jewish families, the Luzzatti spent their life between their home and the synagogue, and were seldom seen elsewhere. They were cultivated people, interested in art and literature, and lived on terms of cordial intimacy with their own employees and workmen, for whom they provided dinner every Sunday. This intercourse was afterwards to have a considerable influence on Luigi Luzzatti's life and outlook.

Luigi Luzzatti was born in Venice on March 1,

[1] Venice is divided into six *sestieri*, or wards.

1841, and his education began in a Jewish private school, but he owed much of his culture to his mother, to whom he was deeply devoted. In politics the family was intensely patriotic, and he was brought up to hate the Austrians, who oppressed his native country. On the outbreak of the revolution of 1848 his elder brother Davide joined the National Guard, Luigi himself being of course too young to take any part in the stirring events of those days. But with the rest of his family he lived through the famous siege of Venice, and when the Austrians and their reactionary vassals recovered from their defeats and swept over the rest of Italy, the Italian tricolour still continued to float above the city of the lagoons. The citizens suffered severe hardships from the Austrian bombardment, famine and cholera. Davide Luzzatti caught the dread disease, and the family had to leave their house, which was too exposed to the enemy shells, and take refuge in a barge. Finally, the heroic resistance was overcome by sheer weight of numbers and hunger, and the city fell once more under the hated Austrian yoke. One of Luigi Luzzatti's first literary efforts was a poem on the return of the Austrians.

In 1850 Luzzatti left the Jewish school to enter the Ginnasio liceale (classical secondary school) of Santa Caterina, afterwards renamed Ginnasio Liceo Marco Foscarini, an excellent institution, where he received a sound education. Among his first teachers were a Jew and a Catholic priest, a combination characteristic of Luzzatti's intellectual upbringing. The former, Mosè Soave, taught him Jewish theology, and aroused in him an interest in religious history in general which he never lost ; the latter, Father Giacomo Zanella, was his instructor in Italian letters. As he records in his memoirs, Luzzatti at the age of eighty was to unveil a monument on the Pincian hill in Rome to his old teacher Zanella, who had first inspired him with a love of Italian literature. Another teacher was Prof. Politeo, to whom he owed his mental evolution. Nor did he neglect sport, and at an early age became proficient in swimming and rowing.

Although brought up in a strictly orthodox Jewish atmosphere, he soon began to have doubts as to the outward profession of his religion, and he ended by becoming in a sense a free-thinker. Yet he never repudiated the faith of his fathers, and was ever ready to protest against the persecution of the Jews. As he wrote many years later, " I am a theist without any particular church, and I defend all who are persecuted for their faith." While still a boy a certain Arminio Wurmbrand mocked at him for being a Jew, whereupon Luzzatti chucked him into the canal ; but when he saw that Wurmbrand could not swim he jumped in after him and pulled him out. Later he had an interesting correspondence with another Jew, Elia Lattes, on the Hebrew religion. In 1861 he reproved a friend who said that as a Jew and an Italian he professed cosmopolitan ideas ; Luzzatti replied that he knew no fatherland but the country in which he was born— Italy—and that the Jews had ceased to be a nation. This was typical of his outlook on Judaism. Nationally he never regarded himself, nor was regarded by others, as anything but an Italian—an unhyphenated Italian, as we should say to-day. But he always professed the deepest respect for the Jewish faith, although he was also keenly interested in other religions, and in his protests against religious persecution he did not forget the Christian Armenians. Years later, when a foreign decoration had been conferred on him and he was asked to fill up a form on receiving the diploma, in the space headed " Religion," he wrote the following words : " By sentiment a Christian, by reason a

Buddhist, for those who accuse me of it a Jew, but advocating the widest toleration of all persuasions."

On completing his school curriculum Luzzatti entered the law faculty of the University of Padua in 1858 ; there he studied under Antonio Messedaglia, who taught economics and statistics, the historian De Leva, and other scholars. Throughout his memoirs he is always alluding with admiration and affection to these men, reminding us of Kipling's poem, " Let us now praise famous men." He was an omnivorous reader, but although he acquired a wide knowledge of literature and history, it was economics which interested him most deeply, and even in his university days he began to devote himself to the study of working-class conditions. He was never impressed by Socialist fantasies, and always rejected the odious theory of class war ; he advocated instead the formation of farmers' associations for the dissemination of a wider knowledge of agriculture among the rural classes. In 1862 he began to hold courses for Venetian youths on economic problems, for he was a firm believer in the necessity of popularising economic study as a reality affecting the everyday life of the citizen and not as mere theory.

In 1863 he took his degree in jurisprudence and for a very short time attended the chambers of Marco Diena, a well-known Jewish lawyer of Venice, a descendant of whom, Giulio Diena, is to-day one of the most noted international lawyers of Italy. But he had no taste for the law as a profession and never practised. He devoted himself instead to economics, with the object of securing a chair of that science and above all of giving practical effect to its dictates as a means for improving the lot of the working masses. His first practical achievement was the founding of a mutual benefit society in Venice, which soon acquired a large membership ; but it fell under the suspicions of the Austrian police, and after the liberation of Venetia in 1866 Luzzatti discovered that criminal proceedings were about to be instituted against him.

He now began to visit various parts of Italy, always with a view to studying working-class conditions and the activities and possibilities of mutual benefit societies ; these interested him from their moral and spiritual side as well as from a purely economic point of view. Mutual benefit societies must, he believed, unite all men as brothers, and " spiritualise the capital of its members." At that time usury played an important and deleterious part in the life of the Italian masses, especially of the small farmers and shopkeepers ; and Luzzatti, like Schulze-Delitsch in Germany, saw in mutual credit the means of combating it. In 1863 he had published a book on credit and people's banks,[1] based on what had been done in Germany, Belgium, and Scotland, with a view to applying these experiences to Italy. He began to conceive an ideal society in which elementary education should be as widely diffused as possible, the industrial spirit generalised, moral principles assimilated by large classes of the population, with a banking system, unlike that of Germany, free of State control.

After taking his degree he was offered several teaching appointments in secondary schools, one at Urbino, where the Jew and free-thinker Luzzatti was preferred to a Catholic priest. But he decided in favour of Milan, where, owing to the higher degree of industrial development and trade activity in the city, he believed that he would have a better opportunity of popularising his ideas on mutual benefit, people's banks, and popular credit. He thus accepted the lectureship of commercial statistics and political economy in the

[1] *La diffusione del credito e le banche popolari.*

Istituto tecnico of Milan at a salary of 1,200 lire a year (£48). His first address was on industrial economics, almost a new subject in Italy. He also held a course of evening classes on social economics for working men. The Sardinian Government had issued its first statistical year-book in 1858, which became that of the Italian Kingdom after 1861, and Luzzatti published a criticism of the methods of this publication, regretting that too little space was devoted in it to the moral and intellectual development and to the industry of the nation, as compared with that assigned to military matters, but he admitted that at that time, when another war against Austria for the liberation of Venice was impending, the army was still the primary consideration for the country.

Luzzatti now undertook a practical campaign in favour of popular credit institutions. His friend Vincenzo Boldrini had planned a labour credit company to operate throughout the whole of Italy, but Luzzatti criticised the scheme, as the country was too large for a single institution of the kind. The " Banca operaia di credito, scambio e lavoro e della piccola industria " of Turin found more favour in his eyes, and in 1864 he held a lecture on popular credit at Lodi, where a people's bank was projected. Tiziano Zalli had drafted the statute of this bank, and Luzzatti suggested certain modifications to it, such as that the rate of interest should not be the same all the year round, but should vary according to the conditions of credit, and this was accepted. The members were at first some 180 small farmers, and the bank eventually became the " Banca popolare agricola di Lodi," and comprised co-operative warehouses among its activities ; it soon developed into a very important institution and came to be regarded as a model for similar banks elsewhere.

His lectures to the Milanese working-men's mutual benefit society on the new forms of co-operation aroused great interest. He spoke on savings banks, popular economics, credit, and other kindred subjects, and the lectures were subsequently published in book form. In an address at Asola, in the province of Mantua, he expounded and compared the three systems for solving the problem of the proletariat—the conventional reactionary system based wholly on charity, the Socialist system aspiring to create a preposterous equality of all men, and that of the Liberal economists, such as Bastiat, Cobden, Bright, Holyoake, Mill, Schulze-Delitzsch, who base themselves on liberty and order and advocate people's banks, co-operative societies, education and moral and economic progress. As Dante says,

> . . . le cose tutte quante
> Han l'ordine tra loro e questo è forma
> Che l'universo a Dio fa simigliante.
>
> (*Paradiso* I. 104–6.)

" The reactionaries," he said, " humiliate you, the Socialists flatter you, whereas it is only by honest work and savings that a splendid future can be prepared for you. Mutual benefit societies assure you a subsidy in case of illness, a pensions fund provides for your old age, workmen's associations enable you to acquire your own homes, co-operative warehouses provide food and other necessaries at a low price." We have a summary of what were to be Luzzatti's activities in after life. As a result of his propaganda and of that of others who advocated his ideas, these associations spread all over Italy, and as early as 1865 he contemplated a federation of people's banks, which materialised in 1876 and flourishes to this day as the " Associazione nazionale ' Luigi Luzzatti ' delle banche popolari co-operative."

Economics did not monopolise the whole of his

activity, for his interest in philosophic and religious studies never flagged. At one time he had thought of founding a rationalist association uniting all who did not profess any definite creed, but who recognised, as he said, " the necessity of prayer through good deeds and the love of all that is beautiful and true." He never abjured the Jewish faith, although he no longer practised it, and he did not become a Christian because he could not get himself to accept the idea of the Divinity of Christ. But he firmly believed in a personal God and in Heaven ; his was more akin to the Unitarianism of the American W. E. Channing than to any other faith.

At this time there were in Italy lively polemics on the suppression of the religious orders. Luzzatti on the whole favoured the measure, because in the struggle for Italian unity still proceeding many of the orders were unfriendly to the national cause. Writing many years later, he admitted that the suppression might have been effected with greater moderation, and he expressed deep admiration for the Franciscan rule, of which in the 'sixties he had known nothing.

Luzzatti's friendships were always many and varied. Among the intimates of his Milan days were the devout Catholic writer Alessandro Manzoni and the Jew Tullio Massarani. On returning to Venice immediately after the departure of the Austrians he met Count Giuseppe Pasolini, then Royal Commissioner in the city and future Minister of Foreign Affairs, and contracted a lasting friendship with him.

In 1866 he was offered the newly created chair of constitutional law at his old university of Padua, but he did not accept it at once, as he was reluctant to leave Milan, where he had contracted so many ties, and it was not until the end of 1867 that he inaugurated his course. The chair was destined to become in a sense a centre of political life in the Veneto, but his lectures were not limited to pure law, as he continued to keep up his interest in economics and sociology, fully realising the close connection between political science and economic life. All his activities, whether as a professor, a writer, a financier, or a Cabinet Minister, were directed to the single object of improving the economic and spiritual conditions of the nation.

Before taking up his duties at Padua, he went to Paris as Italian member of a jury at the great exhibition of 1867 for conferring prizes on men, institutions, and cities which had distinguished themselves in the promotion of good feeling between classes, and of better material, intellectual and moral conditions of the workers. It was a task after his own heart, and in addition to his duties on the jury he set himself to the establishment of commercial connections between the French and Italian peoples' banks, and also to the creation links between the workers of Paris and Milan, although, he was careful to add, these latter contacts were on lines wholly different from those of the *Internationale*, with which he had no sympathy. He cemented many friendships with French economists, such as Léon Say, Paul Leroy-Beaulieu, and Garnier.

On returning to Italy he collaborated with Marco Minghetti, Antonio Scialoja, and Lampertico in founding the Italian Political Economy Society. But he was never a mere theorist, and always tried to give practical expression to his economic ideas ; thus he advocated the creation of a high school of commercial studies in Venice, there being as yet no institution of the kind in Italy. The school actually came into being in 1868 and exists to this day ; among its students many were afterwards to achieve celebrity in business, and also in the diplomatic and consular services.

Luzzatti undertook another task destined to benefit his native city by accepting membership of the Venetian committee for the better utilisation of the newly opened Brenner railway.

Luzzatti was summoned to Florence (then the capital of the Kingdom) in 1869 by Marco Minghetti, Minister of Agriculture, Industry and Commerce, as his General Secretary.[1] The appointment was a political one, usually conferred only on Members of Parliament ; Luzzatti was not in the Chamber, and being under thirty years of age, was not even eligible. Except for a short period after the fall of the Cabinet in 1870, he held the position until 1874 and during his tenure of office he promoted and piloted through Parliament a number of important measures. It was only after being returned for Oderzo for the third time on March 12, 1871, that the Chamber confirmed his election, as he had then reached the age of thirty. He thus initiated his political career as a member of the traditional " Right," the party which ruled Italy from the foundation of the Kingdom in 1861 to 1876. Subsequently, when the new leftward tendencies became fashionable, although frequently in office with men holding those views, Luzzatti never truckled to the demagogic spirit and was ever uncompromising in his hostility to class war. He steadfastly advocated instead a policy of class collaboration, which, as Signor Mussolini said in his commemoration of Luzzatti in the Senate, Fascist legislation is now carrying into effect.

While in office his activity was prodigious. As Italy lacked technical experts for industry, he proceeded, with the support of his chief Minghetti, to create a number of trade schools, and at the same time he did much to promote agricultural education. He was one of the first Italians to realise the injury

---

[1] Corresponding to the rank of Under-Secretary of State.

wrought to agriculture by the destruction of the forests ; he therefore instituted the excellent school of forestry at Vallombrosa, and was able to save what remained of the State forest domain. In later years he was to prove one of the most strenuous and successful advocates of reafforestation. He seldom made excursions into the field of high politics, but he strongly supported Visconti-Venosta's policy for the occupation of Rome in 1870, and was one of the authors of the Law of Papal Guarantees, which survived operated satisfactorily until the Lateran Treaties of 1929. He believed that if the Pope had proved less intractable and had accepted the general principle of the law, its provisions might have been made more liberal and that the State would have renounced the right of intervention in ecclesiastical appointments. But Pius IX rejected the scheme *in toto* and even refused the allowance assigned to him by the Government.

When Luzzatti first entered Parliament he still found there many of the great figures of the Risorgimento, the makers of Italy—Minghetti, Quintino Sella, Baron Ricasoli, Silvio Spaventa, Garibaldi, Correnti, and others. But they were growing old, and with the passing of this heroic age many less desirable men had been returned, party factions were becoming more embittered, and the decay of Parliamentary life had begun. It was to be intensified by the fall of the Right in 1876, by the extension of the suffrage, and to continue in geometrical progression until a wholly new political system was to be ushered in by the events of 1922.

Sella had prepared a Bill instituting the postal savings banks, but although Luzzatti was always ready to support any measure for preserving and fertilising the savings of the people, he hesitated on this occasion, as he feared that the new institutions might prove injurious to the existing people's bank without quite fulfilling their functions. But in the end he was convinced of the merits of the scheme and gave it his full support, only insisting that the rate of interest offered by the postal savings banks should not be so high as to compete unfairly with the others.

There was at the time a conflict of opinion as to whether Italy was destined to remain a purely agricultural country or was capable of industrialisation. Luzzatti maintained that countries wholly dependent on agriculture could never have a complete and flourishing economic life ; they must export their agricultural products to purchase manufactured goods, and as the tendency of all countries (except Great Britain) at that time was towards protection, Italy's farm products were finding ever greater difficulty in securing markets. If, on the other hand, industry also were developed, Italy would be able not only to secure manufactured goods at home, but also to sell her farm products in her own industrial areas when foreign countries closed their doors against them. Luzzatti induced Minghetti to institute a commission of inquiry into Italian industry, with Scialoja as chairman and himself as vice-chairman, until on Scialoja's appointment as Minister of Education he succeeded to the chairmanship. He conducted the most minute investigations into the state of industry, cross-examining employers, traders, and working men all over Italy, which resulted in the enacting of factory laws and other measures both for the protection of the workers and the encouragement of industrial activity.

On the fall of the Cabinet Luzzatti returned to his university chair at Padua. But he remained in close touch with his former chief Minghetti, who had become Premier and who consulted him frequently. He was now a regular contributor to the Milanese economic journal *Il Sole*, and to the *Opinione*, a Roman daily paper edited by Giacomo Dina, on financial and economic problems. In fact, Luzzatti's most valuable contribution to Italian economic life was his unofficial collaboration with Governments and institutions by means of private advice and the Press. He continued to fulfil this task to the very end of his life.

This is how he spent his days at this period. He rose early, he tells us, and began by studying the history of religion ; then he wrote an article for the *Sole* or the *Opinione* and prepared his lectures (at that time he lectured for two hours every day to make up for frequent absences). Lunch followed, and then his university lecture, after which he returned home and worked for two hours on a book he was writing. Dinner ; then an hour's play with his children, and finally reading and study until bedtime at 1 a.m.

Italy's financial situation was then a very critical one. The country was poor, economic activity still lagged, the workers, save in a few favoured spots and trades, were ill paid, badly housed, and inadequately fed. Yet it was necessary to raise money to build up the State and its institutions, without which it was impossible to improve the conditions of the masses and increase the national wealth. In this apparently vicious circle Luzzatti's was always a moderating influence ; he abhorred radical legislation and immature schemes of which his profound knowledge of finance and economics made him see the weak points at once. One of Italy's chief problems was the currency question ; Italy had had to introduce forced paper currency in 1866 and was still suffering from the financial effects of the war of that year. It was due to Luzzatti that this and other financial problems were after many years finally solved. But in spite of his concentration on finance, he saw other aspects of the national situation. When the international horizon was serene he advocated rigid economies, but as soon as dark clouds appeared he was the first to demand measures for strengthening the fighting services.

In the early 'seventies the position might well give cause for anxiety. France was definitely unfriendly ; the Clericals were indignant at Italy's solution of the Roman question and the annexation of Rome, while the Republicans were annoyed because the newly-formed Italian State had chosen a monarchical régime. French public opinion as a whole could not forgive the Italians for not accepting the rôle of humble satellite out of gratitude for French help in 1859. Luzzatti, who was anything but a Francophobe, advised Minghetti to try to strengthen Italy's ties with Germany and Austria, but he was pessimistic, because he distrusted Germany and feared the influence of the ultra-Clerical upper classes in Austria. Yet he felt that the attempt must be made, as the danger from France was the more immediate one. On his advice Minghetti persuaded King Victor Emmanuel to visit Vienna and Berlin in 1873, where he had a most cordial reception. No agreement was then concluded, but the bases of the Triple Alliance were laid, an instrument which proved of use to Italy at the time, as it averted a possible French aggression, although its provisions were to be violated in 1914, and the Central Powers always treated Italy with contempt.

Luzzatti prepared the Milan Economic Congress of May 1875 and proved its leading spirit. The three questions then debated were factory legislation, the protection of emigration, and the fertilisation of the savings of the poorer classes. On the first point Luzzatti, in spite of his admiration for the British economists of the day, had no sympathy for the mill-owner who, while a Liberal and a free-trader, underpaid his workmen and exploited women and children at excessively long hours, but read the lessons in church and subscribed handsomely to mission funds. He was one of the first advocates of sound factory legislation, and in the Chamber he supported the resolutions of the Milan Congress. He first took up the question of the workers in the Sicilian sulphur mines, whose conditions were deplorable, but he would not demand radical factory legislation until he had secured fuller data. He therefore ordered further investigations, after which he carried through measures for insurance against industrial accidents. With regard to emigration he favoured a policy of freedom, but he wished to see emigrants protected against fraud and emigration agents placed under State control ; these views were to materialise in the emigration law of 1901. He continued to encourage popular credit by means of the people's banks, the number of which was 200 by 1882 and 700 by 1892 ; in the early years of the twentieth century the movement suffered a set-back owing to the economic crisis of the time, but it afterwards overcame the difficulties, and in spite of a second set-back due to the World War, the number of these banks had grown to 800 by 1924, sixty years after Luzzatti's first campaign in their favour.

Between 1878 and 1887 Luzzatti's chief task was the revision of the customs tariff, which he carried out three times. In his report on the final revision of 1887 he stated :

> The budget having been balanced at last, the economic factor should take precedence over fiscal considerations. . . . Our object should be to increase the revenue, correct the tariffs, and co-ordinate them more adequately, support the new industries which have arisen since the previous tariff revision, prepare useful negotiations, and defend Italian exports.

It is, in fact, from this date that the export trade received a new impulse. He devoted particular efforts to the development of the iron and steel and mechanical industries, then in their infancy, and Admiral Brin regarded him as his closest collaborator in building up the Italian Navy.

For many years he was chairman of the Budget Committee of the Chamber, and proved a vigilant watch-dog over the finances of the country. In 1891 he entered the Cabinet for the first time as Treasury Minister in the Di Rudinì administration, and was also for a time Finance Minister.[1] He set to work to introduce the most rigid economies and to place the circulation on a sound basis. To achieve this result he had to cut down the appropriations of all his colleagues ; one of them, Pasquale Villari, the Minister of Education, on receiving his request for ruthless economies, wrote to him that this could only be done by introducing into the Ministry an electric machine which would electrocute 2,000 university professors and school teachers, beginning with Villari himself ! He did not neglect his favourite subject of commercial treaties, and he succeeded in concluding a number of them which gave Italy twelve years of tariff peace. He left office on the fall of the Cabinet in 1892, but was again at the Treasury in 1896 under Di Rudinì. During the interval Giolitti had nearly brought Italy's finances to disaster, and it was again Luzzatti who stepped in to restore the situation. He saved the Bank of Naples from collapse, converted the municipal debts of Sicily and Sardinia, implemented his workers' insurance law by an old age pensions fund, and prepared a scheme for giving security to small rural family

---

[1] Until 1923 the Treasury Ministry, which dealt with State financial operations, was separate from that of Finance, which provided for the collection of revenue.

properties. On leaving the Ministry in 1898 he resumed commercial negotiations with France, and succeeded in bringing the ten years' tariff war with that country to an end. He was then made corresponding member of the Institut de France in succession to another great financier, W. E. Gladstone, an honour which he highly prized. The emigration law of 1901 already alluded to and the labour agreements with various countries are largely his work.

In 1903 he returned to the Treasury for the third time ; he effected the conversion of the $4\frac{1}{2}$ per cent. bonds to $3\frac{1}{2}$, and although the more important conversion of the 5 per cent. bonds to 4 was actually carried out by his successor, it was universally recognised that the merit was Luzzatti's. On quitting office in 1906 he resumed his lecture on constitutional law at the University of Rome, to which he had been transferred, and in 1909 he published his great work, *La libertà di conscienza e di scienza*. But he did not neglect his activities in the field of social reform, and it was at this time that he drafted the law on cheap dwellings for the working classes, which proved the foundation for much subsequent legislation. He was leading supporter of the monetary " Latin League," between the States having adopted the franc or its equivalent as the monetary unit, viz. France, Italy, Belgium, Switzerland, and Greece, and he had been the principal negotiator or inspirer of the various monetary conventions on the subject. This was indeed the first attempt of what Luzzatti called monetary world peace. In 1908, after the economic crisis in the United States, he had proposed the creation of an international currency clearing-house, and although the scheme was not adopted, it was raised again at an inter-Allied conference in Paris in 1916, and finally at the Genoa Conference of 1922, but it has not yet materialised. Incidentally Luzzatti contributed to the restoration of the Greek currency at the Latin League conference in Paris in 1909, and was afterwards consulted on currency reform by Turkey and China.

At the end of this same year Luzzatti was again in office, no longer at the Treasury, but at the Ministry of Agriculture, Industry, and Commerce in the Sonnino Cabinet ; this gave him the opportunity of reforming the statistical service, which became a model for other countries, and of creating the Banca del Lavoro. On the resignation of Sonnino early in 1910 Luzzatti became Prime Minister for the first time, and assumed, as was customary, the portfolio of the Interior. Of the measures which he enacted while at the head of the Government we may mention the law for extending employers' liability for accidents to agriculture, the granting of fiscal facilities to co-operative societies, laws against obscene publications, the white slave traffic and cruelty to animals, and various measures for improving the police services. Not less important were his enactments for strengthening the fighting services, especially the law of July 15, 1910, empowering the Government in case of war to enact financial measures without the previous consent of Parliament. He had always opposed the creation of Italian colonies in such distant lands as Eritrea, but he realised the necessity of securing Libya, the last remaining stretch of North Africa not yet occupied by any other great Power, as he felt Italian expansion to be inevitable as well as an historical tradition. He it was who initiated the first preparations for the Libyan expedition which German action in Morocco had rendered urgent, although the actual occupation took place under Giolitti.

Nevertheless, as Premier he was less successful than

in his other activities. He was essentially not a political man of action, and proved incapable of wheedling the warring factions as the craftier and far less scrupulous Giolitti could do, nor could he coerce them with the energy and driving power of a Mussolini. Moreover, he held office at the good pleasure of Giolitti, who did not yet wish to return to Palazzo Braschi,[1] both on account of a sprained angle and because he did not like to tackle a number of awkward problems. He was always, even when out of office, the dominant personality in Parliament, if not in the country ; he had caused Sonnino to fall after a second brief premiership and set up Luzzatti instead, until it should suit his good pleasure to resume the reins of power. Luzzatti, that *animula vagula blandula* of politics, never realised that he was a mere pawn in the wily Giolitti's game. He knew that he had an almost unrivalled grasp of financial and economic problems, and believed that on the strength of these very real qualities he could hold his own even as a Prime Minister amid the treacherous quicksands of Monte Çitorio.[2] But he had not perhaps that vision of the political situation as a whole which is necessary for a Prime Minister, and his essentially kindly nature and absence of guile or sense of hatred prevented him from acting with that ruthless vigour which is so often indispensable in high places. Thus as soon as Giolitti saw fit to return he pressed the Parliamentary button and Luzzatti fell.

Luzzatti now resumed those other activities in which he was really pre-eminent. On the outbreak of the World War he was one of the few Italian statesmen of the old school who saw the international situation in its true light. Although he had been, as we have

---

[1] The Ministry of the Interior, which was then also the Prime Minister's office.
[2] The Parliament building.

seen, one of the early supporters of the Triple Alliance, he realised in July 1914 that its provisions had been violated by Austria, and that Italy could not be dragged into the struggle against the Entente at the heels of the Central Powers. Once Italy had broken away from the Triplice and declared her neutrality, he knew that intervention on the other side was merely a question of time. Luzzatti, we must remember, was a Venetian, and had not forgotten Austrian rule. He proved a true patriot, and did not hesitate to break with many lifelong friends who had been deceived by the neutralist, pro-German, and defeatist propaganda. The Parliament which finally accepted Salandra's interventionist policy was in its majority Giolittian and neutralist, and only gave the Premier its support because of the overwhelming wave of public opinion outside Parliament in his favour. Luzzatti conducted an active war propaganda and was untiring in his encouragement to the nation to fight on until victory was achieved. He was equally emphatic in his support of inter-Allied solidarity, for he had been, as we have seen, an unswerving friend of Great Britain and France, especially of Great Britain, whose history he knew more intimately than many Englishmen. He devoted himself to all forms of war activity and relief work, promoted the foundation of the national fund for the orphans of peasants who had been killed in action and became its chairman. When a large part of his beloved Veneto had been invaded after Caporetto he was appointed Government Commissioner for the relief of the refugees, and after the final victory of Vittorio Veneto he successfully advocated the creation of a credit institute for the reconstruction of the devastated areas both within and without the old frontiers. Much has been heard of the reconstruction of the French devastated area, but little of what was done in the smaller but not less terribly war-wasted Veneto, and much of the merit for this work is Luzzatti's. Although he was not a member of the Italian Peace Delegation, he proved a vigorous supporter of the Italian position in the protracted and often unseemly wrangles over the Adriatic, and had a heated correspondence with Clemenceau on Italy's claims.

In the post-war period he was for a short time (March–June 1920) again at the Treasury in the last of Nitti's short-lived and unfortunate administrations. During the Premier's absence at the Peace Conference he was Vice-President of the Cabinet, and showed energy in facing the revolutionary railwaymen's strike in May. With the final fall of Nitti Luzzatti's active political career ended. But he continued his valuable work of giving sound advice on financial and economic problems, while keeping himself in the background. Minister after Minister applied to him for counsel, and he always gave it freely and willingly. In fact, he enjoyed his position of high-priest of finance and economics, whom all consulted, but who no longer appeared in the public eye. Even when he disagreed with his interlocutors his disagreement was without bitterness, for bitterness was alien to his nature. " Let us disagree," he said, " for dissent is a necessity ; but let us temper dissent with the love of country and may the name of Italy effect between us the same miracle of inexhaustible affection which made Virgil and Sordello embrace."

From the first moment of the advent of Fascism, although the movement was in such sharp contrast with the tradition of Parliamentary and political Italy which he had always known, and although at his age it must have been difficult to visualise such a radical transformation, yet he at once sensed its value for the betterment of the economic conditions of the Italian people, and he collaborated silently but effectively

with the new leaders. He strongly supported De
Stefani's measures for restoring the financial situation ;
he collaborated with Belluzzo, the Minister of National
Economy, to save the organisation of popular credit
and to reform the professional schools and the forest
service ; with Dino Alfieri for the reorganisation of
the co-operative societies, which had been shaken to
their foundations by the abuses introduced by the
Socialist administrators inspired solely by the spirit of
class war ; with Rossoni for the extension of cheap
dwellings, and with Volpi in the stabilisation of the
currency, urging on him the necessity of gradualising
the policy of deflation. From time to time he would
write short articles, sometimes merely notes, for the
Corriere della Sera, on his favourite topics, and each
of them contained a sound practical idea which often
found expression in the measures afterwards enacted
by the Government.

Luzzatti spent the last years of his life in Rome in
his flat in Via Veneto, ever working and reading in a
large well-lighted room, containing little furniture except five huge tables each piled high with books,
pamphlets, newspapers, cuttings, MSS. in many
languages, apparently in hopeless confusion. But in
the course of discussion he would suddenly plunge into
one of those wildernesses of paper and extract what he
wanted to illustrate some point of his argument. He
was in appearance, and he was indeed regarded both
by Italians and foreigners, as the Patriarch, the Grand
Old Man of economics. The stream of callers was
ceaseless. Princes of the Blood, Italian and foreign
diplomats, Cabinet Ministers, men of all political views
and beliefs were among his visitors. He was particularly glad to receive the humblest people, especially
those who wished to constitute themselves into a mutual
benefit club, and those who wanted his help—em-

ployers, workers, railwaymen—for the foundation of a cheap dwelling association. Russian princes ruined by the revolution, British Labour M.P.s, U.S. bankers, deputations of orphans of peasants killed in action, monsignori, rabbis, Protestant clergymen, French economists, German journalists, Finns, who had not forgotten how he had raised his voice in defence of the University of Helsingfors which the Tsarist Government had tried to Russify, the Capitani Reggenti of San Marino, committees representing peoples' banks, Indian or Egyptian co-operatives who came to consult him on agricultural credit for the benefit of ryots and fellahs, authors of works on Franciscan studies, followed by woollen manufacturers from Biella or silk spinners from Lombardy, promoters of reafforestation schemes, the Norwegian Minister anxious to obtain advice as to the best means of converting the Norwegian debt : all these and many others did he receive.

Franciscans and Capuchins were particularly welcome ; they came to ask him to support their petitions to the Fondo per il Culto [1] for their missions abroad, for the rebuilding of churches in the devastated area, for getting back those convents suppressed in the years of conflict between Church and State. He never refused them his support, and a petition recommended by him was almost sure of favourable consideration. The Dominicans were less welcome, for Luzzatti could never dissociate them in his mind from the memories of the Inquisition, which to him was absolute anathema ; those memories even affected his views on Spain, for which country he never felt any interest.

What he never forgot was his reprobation of the persecution of the Jews and the Armenians. Although,

---

[1] A State fund formed of the property of the suppressed religious bodies ; its revenues are expended on religious objects formerly provided for by the suppressed bodies.

as we have seen, no longer a professing Jew—he re-garded the Jewish faith as too antiquated and divorced from present-day conditions—and without sympathy for Zionism, he had a deep regard for the Jewish people, and took a great interest in their history and their beliefs, and he abhorred all forms of persecution. He had frequently raised his voice to protest against the action of the Russian and Rumanian Governments, and as early as the time of the Berlin Congress of 1878 he insistently demanded the insertion of clauses in the treaty for the protection of the Rumanian Jews. His action in this field culminated in 1913–14, when during the negotiations for peace in the Balkans, he pressed on Bratianu to grant full civil rights to the Jews in Rumania, One day, after the war, a Polish statesman called on him, and Luzzatti interrupted his complimentary speech with the words, " Soyez bon avec les Juifs." The Pole replied : " C'est qu'ils font du fracas à l'étranger. Nous en Pologne, nous ne nous en apercevons même pas." To which Luzzatti retorted : " C'est toujours la même chose : les persécuteurs ne s'aperçoivent jamais des persécutions qu'ils infligent."

His interest in the Armenians was almost as keen as that in the Jews. When a Turkish statesman called on him one day, he warmly recommended the Armenians to him, adding that, on the outbreak of the Turkish revolution of 1908, he had expressed sympathy with the Young Turks, and that, when later they had proved as ruthless towards the Armenians and other opponents as had Abdul Hamid, and he, Luzzatti, had been blamed in Italy for having defended the new Turkish régime, he had replied : " Is it my fault that '89 has been followed by '92 ? " It was at Luzzatti's house that the scheme for creating the village of Nor-Arax was inaugurated to house Armenian refugees who were given work in making Oriental carpets ; for this undertaking he secured the support of Signor Mussolini and the Ministers of Communications and Finance, and to-day Nor-Arax is a flourishing model community where every family has its own house and vegetable garden and assured employment, with a church, a school, and recreation grounds.

Luzzatti when I knew him was a typical figure of late nineteenth-century Italy, although always open to new ideas. He did not have a particularly Jewish cast of countenance. He then had sparse white hair, eyes deeply set under shaggy eyebrows, and a little Imperial beard—the famous *pizzetto* of the caricatures. He was indeed, after Giolitti and Ernesto Nathan, also a Jew, who had been for several years Mayor of Rome, the most frequently caricatured man in Italy. With all his many admirable qualities he had his little weaknesses, of a kind which provide good material for the comic press. He had a tendency to rhetoric, due perhaps to his deep sincerity and to his unswerving conviction in the merits of the causes he was supporting. While his kindly nature prevented him from bitter criticisms of men whom he knew to be inferior to himself, he did not hesitate to show that he was fully conscious of the value of his own work and of the depth of his knowledge and insight. This of course lent itself to caricature and parody, and for many years the *Travaso*, the most amusing comic paper in Italy, simply battened on Luzzatti. He liked above all to be consulted by foreigners. On the occasion of Lloyd George's famous " people's budget " in 1909, an important London Conservative organ instructed its correspondents abroad to interview the leading foreign experts on the measure. The Rome correspondent of the paper called on Luzzatti, who, although not then in the Government, at first showed unwillingness to express any opinion, as he might be called upon again to take office. But the journalist, who knew Luzzatti well, said : " I have not come to your Excellency as to the former and future Treasury Minister, nor to the future Premier of Italy, but to the greatest financier and economist in Europe." To which Luzzatti replied : " Perhaps in that case I might grant you a short expression of my views." He thereupon opened a drawer and presented his English friend with a full interview already written.

Luzzatti had been created Minister of State, a highly prized honorary position, in 1906. He died on March 29, 1927.

In commemorating him in the Chamber of Deputies, the former Finance Minister, Alberto De Stefani, like Luzzatti a professor turned expert of the highest eminence, said that his late colleague could not be called a financier, an economist, a political man, a philosopher ; he had all the possibilities, because in him realism operated in all its fullness. " His mind was predisposed to succeed to vast heritages—of Quintino Sella, Angelo Messedaglia, Marco Minghetti—and he absorbed them in himself in a dignified fusion in which knowledge and passion fertilise each other, and define and limit themselves. Had he lived in England, he would have been among the representative men of the Victorian age ; in Italy, by the happy combination in him of many qualities and the measure and harmony with which he gave expression to them, he represented the whole race. . . . He served his faith in the divine order, his country and the idea of human brotherhood with a pure heart and with a power to rise above his surroundings, with a fire which was never extinguished. If he who loves things for themselves and not for himself is great, he was surely a great man. That idea of brotherhood gave political inspiration and forms of gentleness to his action, and it was also the measure and the substance of his political thought. But he was with us in the higher interest of the country, for he understood its necessities."

In the Senate, Luzzatti was eloquently commemorated by Signor Mussolini himself. The Duce said that in the past few years he had been in close touch with Luzzatti. "He had the courtesy often to come to Palazzo Chigi to discuss the questions which interested him most deeply—public savings, State finance, prudential societies, co-operation, the orphans of peasants fallen in the war whose fate he had so greatly at heart. Often the conversation drifted from the question at issue to the sphere of ideas. In spite of the difference in age and temperament, Luigi Luzzatti had grasped the strength and inevitable realism of Fascism. His last public expressions were of full support for the financial and economic policy of the Government. I regarded his suggestions, his advice, his approval as of the highest value.

"Luigi Luzzatti," the Duce concluded, "was a wise man in the ancient and classical meaning of the word. He had sailed over all the seas and oceans of human knowledge ; nor did his ship ever risk being wrecked on the shallows of scepticism and negation, for he believed firmly, and faith is a reliable compass for all ideal voyages. A wise man and a believer at the same time, therefore drawn towards toleration, indulgence, and goodness, he was, and he could not have been otherwise, intensely optimistic. This sometimes led him to a roseate vision of life which made him feel the painful discordance of these iron times so full of contrasting egoisms, of fierce political, economic, financial, intellectual rivalries, whereby human nature seems more ferocious than ever, its ferocity aggravated by hypocrisy and cynicism.

" But it is necessary, if the great spiritual balance of the peoples is to be restored, that even ' the wise and good men ' should exist, men who above the clash of conflicting interests remind us of the eternal truths, without which the struggle of man against man, of all against all, would end in savage chaos and in the decline of all civilisation.

" Luigi Luzzatti enters into the ranks of these wise, agile, and pure intellects which in all times honour their country ; it is just that their country should deplore his disappearance and honour him."

LUDWIG MOND
By Hector Bolitho

Ludwig Mond

LUDWIG MOND

BY HECTOR BOLITHO

Two years ago, when I was asked to write the biography of Alfred Mond, the first Lord Melchett, I was given the keys of a mahogany desk which had not been opened for many years. In his busy life Alfred Mond had never bothered to unlock it, although he knew that it contained the papers of his family, telling their story from late in the eighteenth century : the story of four generations of German Jews, fighting to free themselves of anti-Semitic oppression. They rose from the poverty and obscurity of a small Hessian farming village, to influence and riches, by sheer force of character. I cannot forget the calm July afternoon in Lord Melchett's London house, when I unlocked the desk and turned over the letters and papers from which I was to write the story. It began with the persecuted, half-blind little shopkeeper of Ziegenhain at the end of the eighteenth century and the drunken soldiers who raided his shop and left him melancholy and poor. The old man conquering his depression and, in the last, fine vigour of his manhood, going out and finding a new wife so that he might have a son to pray for him when he was dead. He was more than sixty then. Then the son growing to manhood and tramping the road into Cassel, to be apprenticed to Levinsohn, a cultivated Jew who made the dresses for the Court Theatre. The marriage to Levinsohn's daughter, and, as the years passed, their son, the third generation of which we have record, crossing the Channel for the fuller freedom of life in England. This was Ludwig Mond, father of Alfred Mond, and grandfather of the present Lord Melchett.

155

He was to be no more than the background of my biography ; the father of the subject of my interest. From the first day when I opened the desk of old papers, Ludwig Mond held my affection and my interest : the great figure, seared by experience, mighty with character, radiant with talent. Only biographers and historians can know the sensations of discovering the character of a dead man through his papers. It leads to a knowledge of him so intimate that the mind and judgment of the dead man become as real to one as if he were still alive and admitted to one's friendship. In Cassel there is a small but splendid collection of pictures in the public gallery : some of the finest Rembrandts in Germany. Ludwig Mond, too, might have been born for Rembrandt to paint, for only Rembrandt would have discovered and revealed the fierce battle within the scientist, the battle which brought the final victory to a Jewish family, struggling out of the German social and economic persecution, to the ease and honour of British citizenship. It was Ludwig Mond's character and achievement which held me with the fascination of a great portrait or great novel. One was drawn into reading his letters with something of the fascination of the beginning of *Madame Bovary* or *Wuthering Heights*. There was such richness in Ludwig Mond's story that I was afraid lest, in spite of myself, the life of the son would be overshadowed by the life of the father, by reason of the queer hypnosis which I experienced.

Ludwig Mond's blood was Jewish : his immediate background was that of a middle-class Jewish family, enjoying good conversation, music, and books, drinking good wine, and harbouring friends with charm and talent. As far as we can trace them, before Ludwig's parents, the Monds had risen as a typical Jewish family, beginning as pariahs in a village of bigoted, suspicious, and ignorant German peasants. The first sign of their intellectual and social emancipation came in the house in Cassel, where Ludwig Mond lived as a child. In the beginning he revealed the three great forces which dominated him to the end—courage, scientific curiosity, and truth. They were manifest when he was still a little boy—when he was " a fine little fellow with dark brown eyes and golden-brown hair."

When he was five years old, Ludwig punished a boy for being cruel to a playfellow in the street. Then he found his way alone to the barber's shop and asked that his hair should be cut off. He did not wish to look like a little girl. One day, when he was seven years old, he sat at his mother's feet, watching her dark-brown, artificial curls, and the restless needle in her hand. He frowned, with the first glimmer of a scientist's inquiry, and he asked her what became of the wool when a hole was worn in a stocking. About the same time an aunt came to the house and said, " Dear Ludwig, what am I ? " She expected the answer, " My dear Auntie." Ludwig was already struggling against humbug. He muttered " Garstig " (ugly), and went on with his play.

These three little stories reveal all of his character. It never changed. It only grew until courage, scientific curiosity, and truth were torrents within him.

In subdued measure these were also the qualities in Ludwig Mond's mother. Indeed, the father fades and becomes colourless when we trace Ludwig's inheritance of character. In the main, it was Levinsohn blood and not Mond blood that made Ludwig great. The mother, a cultivated, gentle, wise woman, was the guide of Ludwig's childhood just as she was the source from which he drew most of his virtues. When Ludwig was seventeen he was studying under Bunsen in

Heidelberg. He had already attracted attention as a student in Marburg. We can turn to two letters written to him by his mother while Ludwig was in Heidelberg and find the key to their relationship and to their mutual strength. She wrote :

" Suit yourself to all you hear, but do not build your opinions accordingly. That is Jewish ill-breeding. Accept the thoughts that are given to you, work on them, and only after ripe consideration, form your own opinion. Have forethought in choosing your associates. . . . I wish that my children may learn much. I cannot leave behind for them more than their knowledge and a good heart. Herewith I send a lamp, vest, washing, some meat, and a piece of birthday cake. When the lamp burns upon your table, it will make you feel at home."

Ludwig accepted the moral laws of his mother. His father did not seem to matter very much : he was a disgruntled, angry man, suspicious of Ludwig's learning because he had little himself. But the mother was the dominant force. Nor were all her anxieties material or ethical : the spirit of the Jews was strong in her. She sent Ludwig some " Matzen " and with it a letter :

". . . When you are eating the ' Matzen,' please remember the deliverance of your forefathers from the pressure and restraint of dreadful slavery."

She dreamed of Ludwig's escape and his rise to honour. Within a year of his joining Bunsen's classes, he was recognised as a young scientist of promise. He had already broken down the racial barriers of Heidelberg by being elected to the Corps Rhenania, one of the most exclusive duelling and Social Corps in the University. Bunsen was delighted by his pupil : he leaned over him in the laboratory and encouraged him. Away from the chemist's bench, Ludwig became a skilled duellist, and he wrote the names of his many conquests within the guard of his rapier! Thus far, his mother was pleased. But she continued to recall the deliverance of the Jews " from the pressure and restraint of dreadful slavery." She sought for still greater security for her son.

The story of the great Benjamin Disraeli was already known in Cassel. He was a Jew, no more noble in origin than the Levinsohns and Müllers, from whom Henrietta Mond drew her blood. Indeed, the Christian name Müller had been given to one of her ancestors by the Landgraf as a reward for saving his son from drowning in a pond. The Aryan name was to help them in their fight against persecution. Henrietta Mond felt no qualms when she contemplated Disraeli's achievement. Ludwig too should be an Englishman. There was no reason why her son should suffer in the darkness of German resentment if England was willing to welcome clever Jews and offer them kindliness, opportunity, and honour. During the first years of her reign, Queen Victoria had gone into the City of London and she had bestowed a baronetcy upon a Jew. In the country of such compassionate people, Ludwig might come to the honour and greatness his talents deserved. Ludwig was already betrothed to his cousin, Frida. She too saw the dawn of his opportunity. She wrote: " I write this with a trembling hand, but it must be said . . . England is the land for you."

In 1866 Ludwig Mond began his battle in Lancashire. He was young, strong, and talented. Honours had already come to him in Utrecht and Heidelberg, and his sulphur-recovery process had been adopted by sixty licensees. He was married and,

with his wife, he had settled into a house called " The
Hollies," which looked out over an open field in Farnworth.   Ludwig had his scientific secret—the secret
of the soda process—in his hands. It was to be
the foundation of his fortune. He had domestic
security and he had his indomitable courage with
which to conquer the suspicious Lancashire men. At
first they did not understand the broad-shouldered
German with his black hat, his black coat, and his
foreign accent. He walked arrogantly, with a swing
which made it seem that the path belonged to him.
His wife spoke little English, and when the butcher
came to the door she once had to call Ludwig from
his room to speak to him. In the morning, before
Ludwig set out for the works, which were some miles
away, she would sit at the window with him, combing
his long hair, so that all passers-by could see. In the
first months they had few friends. Frida wrote to
her mother : " The English say ' My house is my
castle,' but they ought to add to that, ' and I am
locked up in it.' "

The Englishmen slowly came out of their castles.
They had respect for strength and Ludwig impressed
them : his self-confidence was supported by ideas. Of
his strength they were already assured. One night,
in the little club at Widnes, he had opened his shirt
and he had thumped his chest. The Lancashire men
had been intimidated and they had listened to him in
awe. He was a Socialist, he told them. His inventions were to be for the mass of the people. He would
build great factories

in steel and stone—towers and steel rails, floor upon floor
of immortal strength, and within, he would make a dream
come true. A dream of action and invention : the secrets
of nature wrested from her—made obedient by mankind for
its own enlargement and happiness. . . . Ludwig Mond,

in his black coat and his monstrous black hat, became a wonder in the land.

This is more the story of Ludwig Mond the Jew than Ludwig Mond the chemist and manufacturer. When we seek for the apparent evidences of Jewry in him, we are disappointed. He must be considered in relation to his forebears and to his sons before we can discover his place in this story of a German-Jewish family, rising to riches in England. His father and his grandfather before him were devout Jews. His mother, too, as we have seen, sent him " Matzen " to Heidelberg, to remind him of the deliverance of his forefathers. This for his forebears. His son, Alfred Mond, embraced Zionism towards the end of his life with naïve and fierce sincerity, after an education and career which were almost estranged from Jewish interests. Ludwig's grandson and granddaughter, within recent months, have plunged finally into Jewry by embracing the religion as well as the obligations of race. But, between the first Monds and this violent change in the living family, Ludwig Mond stands, almost an agnostic—certainly a man who believed in the slow grinding process of building up character, without the need for divine inspiration. His children were not confirmed as Jews or Christians. Yet the violence of Jewry was so strong in their blood that one of them devoted his life and his fortune to Jewry, when, at last, he saw the light of the Zionists' dream radiant over the fields of Palestine.

Ludwig Mond was not interested in causes. He was an individualist, dealing with men as individuals. He was the champion of humanity, but not of the opposed bands of zealots into which humanity divides itself. His encouragement and charity were given in equal measure to Christians and Jews and unbelievers.

11

When I was gathering stories of his early life among the old people who knew him at Farnworth, two pictures were given to me : they sum up all his attitude towards poor or humble people. They are a key also to his conduct when he came to control thousands of workmen towards whom, as an employer, he accepted a moral responsibility unique in the last century.

On the eve of the great change, when he was going from his modest house in Farnworth to the mansion at Winnington, he was busy upon the plans for the immense plant in which his sulphur recovery process was to be worked. Sitting at his desk, he heard the sounds of a woman in distress. It was the poor extra servant who had been dismissed because the Monds were leaving the village. Ludwig looked up from his plans and he sent for the woman. He asked her what she intended doing and, amazed at being summoned by the big man of whom she had been afraid, she said that she supposed that she must trust in God.

" Nonsense, you won't have to do that," he said. " You can take in washing."

The woman said she had no place in which to wash clothes. Ludwig went back to his desk and, sweeping all thoughts of the Winnington works aside, he planned a perfect wash-house, with labour-saving devices. The wash-house was their present to the servant when the Monds left Farnworth for Winnington. When the first Christmas came in England, Ludwig gave each of his servants an orange. They went home with a poor idea of German generosity, but when they bit the oranges, there was a sovereign in each of them.

Here was the kindness in the busy man. But it was never sentimental or divorced from the practical. When he was asked to present a prize for competition among the cyclists in his works, he said, " How much is a bicycle ? " " Twenty pounds," he was told.

" All my men cannot buy bicycles. But they've all got feet. I shall give the prize, but let them run for it." And he insisted that they should start scratch.

Can these few hurried pictures give any impression of the brave man who closed the little house at Farnworth, to buy and live in the mansion of the Stanleys of Alderley at Winnington ? Can they suggest the indomitable courage of the man who set out, in company with John Brunner, to build the greatest soda process works in the world, with little capital, and the resentment of both the gentry and workers in the country about them ? The first were appalled at the intrusion of chemical works into one of their loveliest parks. The latter were suspicious of the foreigner and, with typical Lancashire stubbornness, they refused to work for him. In the beginning, Ludwig Mond had to engage Irish harvesters to change the peaceful park into a forest of chimneys, towers and blazing furnaces.

The quiet place in which Ruskin had talked, where the Stanleys of Alderley had lived, estranged from such vulgarities as industry and progress, suffered a revolution in Ludwig Mond's hands. The house itself was treated tenderly. No error of taste disturbed its beauty. But around it the factories grew, and in them the workmen struggled, buoyed up by Ludwig's encouragement and force, to perfect his process.

In 1878 the rewards came to him. Ludwig had slaved for six years, fighting the sparsity of capital, the faults in his process, and the apathy of the markets. But, in 1878, the output of soda was trebled, and each ton brought a profit of one pound. Still Ludwig allowed himself no rest. His house was in the centre of the works. At night he slept with a long bell-rope hanging out of his window so that any workman could summon him from his sleep. If the bell-rope was pulled, Ludwig Mond would jump from his bed, and with a big dressing-gown wrapped about him, he would run over to the works. There would be a complication in the machinery or, on rare occasions, a man might be hurt or burned. Then Frida Mond would join her husband, with oil and brandy and linen. Once she came back to the house to tear up the sheet from her bed into long bandages.

> In her gentle way, she lent every aid to the robust Ludwig. People said that they were like an eagle and a dove.

The story of Ludwig Mond's achievements as a chemist has been told many times. He was honoured in almost every country in Europe and, in England, respect came to him, not only for his achievements, but also for his character. Jews are frequently accused of being flamboyant. An Oriental love of gilt and colour sometimes bursts in when they have possessions. It is said that the pretentious and innocently vulgar appeal to them readily. Ludwig Mond was never pretentious or vulgar, in the days of his riches, nor did he ever cease to be a subdued man of taste, an employer beloved by his workmen, a scholar and collector of pictures respected by his contemporaries.

I want to dismiss the record of his great work as a scientist and concentrate only on the effect it had upon him as a man. He made a vast fortune when he was still young enough to enjoy what pleasure it could bring to him. The nearest he ever came to a grand house in London was " The Poplars," in Avenue Road, where he still worked in a laboratory, and where he collected the nucleus of the Mond collection of pictures, now in the National Gallery. As an employer, he astounded other employers by introducing the eight-hour day at a time when the emancipation of the workman was still a dream in the minds of a few brave enthusiasts. He even introduced annual holidays and, perhaps for the first time in the history of industry and labour in England, working men went for their holidays to the seaside. The advantages and reforms which have been achieved elsewhere only since the Great War were introduced into Ludwig Mond's chemical works in the 'eighties and 'nineties of the last century. He was humane without being sentimental. When a workman suddenly fell at his feet from a great height, Ludwig bent over him and said, " My poor man, are you hurt ? " The man stood up and said, " No." " Then get on with your work " was Ludwig's only comment as he walked away.

In the 'eighties Ludwig Mond was a rich man. But he never plunged into new excesses or luxuries : he merely developed the tastes which had been with him from the beginning. Even in Winnington, where the great factories pressed in against his house, there was music and there was good conversation. Painters came and stayed with him ; musicians were his friends. But the fullness of his happiness came to him in Rome. One day, Ludwig and his wife were walking through the streets of Rome : they came to the Spanish steps. Ludwig paused to buy her some anemones in the flower market : then they climbed up together, until they paused at the summit of the steps, to look back over Rome. They walked towards the Via Sistina, and there, on the corner, the house of their dreams was waiting for them : the Palazzo of Zuccari, which the painter had built out of the money he had brought back from England, after painting Elizabeth and her Court. The house was empty. The frescoes Zuccari had painted were still on the walls, and from the balcony Frida and Ludwig Mond could look out over the brown roofs of Rome, towards the arched dome of St. Peter's. This was to be their home in Italy. They bought it eagerly, like children. They would not buy their pictures in the stuffy auction rooms of London. Here, escaping for a little time each year, they would gather together all the beautiful things they could find. And here their friends would come.

The buying of the house in Rome was a significant new light upon Ludwig Mond. Other great industrialists had risen with him in England. They were already filling the fine houses of London with Leightons and Tademas, and they were already coveting the peerages which England so discreetly gives to those foreigners who are willing to enrich her. Neither the honours nor the social achievements affected Ludwig Mond. He only saw his old life in fuller colours. There was to be no change, no pandering to a social system. Ludwig Mond's friends in Rome were people who painted or those who were unearthing the buried glory of the Forum. D'Annunzio was his neighbour and friend ; Duse came to talk with them—Siegfried Wagner and the young Marconi, to whom Ludwig was especially attracted because of the eager inquiry of his mind.

As the works at Winnington filled Ludwig Mond's pockets, so he turned his gold into treasures. Titians and a fine Tintoretto were hung on his walls ; Paul Veronese, Liberale da Verona and Correggio—and the beautiful Filippo Lippi which is now in Signor Mussolini's collection, hanging in the Palazzo Venezia.

In the gardens behind the palazzo Ludwig built a hall, especially for music. Here the less-known works of Bach were performed in the cool evenings. Nothing ugly or meretricious came near to Ludwig Mond, just as nothing ugly or meretricious came from him. One pauses, in a flash of self-criticism, to wonder if too much adulation is being poured upon his character. And then, in justice to the reader, one turns to find

Ludwig Mond's faults. They were few. A certain ruthlessness marred the relationship with his second son, Alfred. A certain intolerance for any character which was not the same as his own. Having few weaknesses, he did not understand weakness in others. Nor did he understand worldly ambition, pursued for its own sake. Ludwig Mond saw his great inventions, which had changed the standard of domestic hygiene in England, through cheap soap, glass, and paper, in relation to humanity. He worked for mankind and for the satisfaction of the violent sense of necessity within himself. Perhaps there was another fault which was apparent only to those who came near to him. He was impatient of the vagaries of female character ; impatient of those who did not obey his own rule of thought and discipline. It did not prevent him from being tender, for his heart often ruled him when his reason made him intolerant. One loves no picture of him more than the scene at the time of the birth of his grandchild. He had delayed his departure for Rome, so as to be in London when the baby was born. The baby did not arrive as early as was expected and Ludwig, rising to the noble old form of his earlier days, was discovered stamping up and down the office, fretful over the delay, mumbling to himself, " In all their lives, women have only one calculation to make and they always get it wrong."

Ludwig was, perhaps, intolerant of his second son. The elder son, now Sir Robert Mond, came more easily within Ludwig Mond's comprehension. He was purely a scholar and a scientist. His manner was easy and his mind was near to his father's understanding. But Alfred Mond was a lonely figure, conscious of certain personal disadvantages which caused him to be on the defensive with those who came near to him. The difference between the two sons and the attitude of the father towards them can be traced in the story of the years when Alfred and Robert Mond were at the University. The older son was a musician, but Alfred played little other than poker. Sometimes Ludwig regretted the difference between his sons. He would walk up and down, the tassel of his nightcap shaking and showing his agitation. If he opened one door, he would hear the restrained calm of a Bach fugue being played by Robert. If he opened the other door, he found Alfred and his friends playing poker. Again and again he would say, " My God—Bach and poker ! They are different boys indeed."

He did not realise that Alfred was arrested in his growth. His tastes were no less fine than those of his brother, but they flowered slowly. Indeed, Alfred's taste was perhaps more experimental, and it was not until he discovered the new Wagner that he became fully interested in music. Then it was that the poker cards were put away. Ludwig Mond walked up and down again. This time he had to listen to Alfred singing Wolfram's aria from *Tannhäuser*, " *O ! Du mein holder Abendstern.*" Alfred's fingers were stiff as drumsticks, and his dearest friends would not have accused him of any beauty in his voice. This time Ludwig changed his complaint. " Oh, God ! Oh, God ! If he would only play poker. I like poker better than Wagner."

If there was intolerance, it was for those who were near to him and from whom he had a right to expect only the best. For his workmen he had understanding and compassion. When he had been a slip of a boy in Cassel, he had said to his mother, that he would " prepare and educate workmen, and care for them ; that they should have a pleasant and comfortable home." She had never forgotten the young promise and she had reminded him of it, again and again. He kept the promise, for no works in the length and breadth of the land were as contented as the Brunner Mond works at Winnington. It was in 1889 that they introduced the eight-hour day. The relationship between master and man was extraordinary. Ludwig would have been indignant if he had been suspected of weakness in his kindness. Once, with a twinkle in his eye, he had said, in discussing some new machinery, that the machinery would cost two thousand pounds. " When machinery wears out, I must replace it at great cost. But if six men wear out, I can sack them and get new ones." He hated to be thought kind, and he trusted and he expected to be trusted. Once when he was at Winnington he walked through the works and found a man sitting down. The man leapt to his feet. " Sit down," said Ludwig Mond, " I know you would not be resting if your work were not finished."

Such a figure and character must have seemed strange and inspiring to the British working man of the day. In our own time, when the Jews have attracted the attention of the world to their racial perplexities by reason of the situation in Germany, Ludwig Mond provides us with an interesting example. The Jewish problem has never been the same for England as for Germany, but our tolerance for oppressed minorities is justified in men like Ludwig Mond. Indeed, since foreigners always suspect us of shrewd, material motives in our high moral purposes, we are proved to be the gainers in the end. For men of Ludwig Mond's character and talent enrich our industry, and they maintain and extend our culture. Ludwig Mond was cultivated by instinct and not merely through fortune and success. The success of

his inventions did not seem to touch him. Ludwig
Mond was born to sit over his bench, discovering the
processes by which science was mastered : not the
processes by which fortunes and honour were achieved.
Experiment was his passion. Honours were poured
upon him. He went to Heidelberg, where he had
been a student under Bunsen. His faith in Ludwig
had been justified. The master was dead now and
there was a new professor to greet Ludwig. And the
University honoured him with a degree. Oxford and
Manchester followed by making him Doctor of Literature and Doctor of Science respectively. He was
elected President of the Society of Chemical Industry,
which he had helped to form, and he was a Fellow of
the Royal Society. His fame brought honours from
other countries. Padua made him a Doctor of Science,
Rome elected him to the Reale Accademia dei Lincei.
He was elected to the German Chemical Society, the
Prussian Academy of Science, and the Royal Society
of Naples. He was given the Grand Cordon of the
Crown of Italy. He never sought or coveted an English title. His eldest son was to be knighted, his second
son was to be a peer, but Ludwig was too faithful to
what was within him, the self-criticism, the pursuit,
the excitement of his science, to care. Therein lay
his greatness. He died with all the talents with which
he was born. Courage, passion for scientific experiment, and truth. All three were enriched through his
experience. Somebody who remembers him has said :
" I never thought of money in connection with Ludwig
Mond, and yet I knew him for many years. It was
always evident that he was a man of taste and knowledge, but it was never in any way apparent that he
was a rich man. Precious things gathered about him
because they belonged to him ; not because the accident of fortune made it possible for him to buy them."

In 1897 Ludwig was still at his experimental bench. He had his palazzo in Rome and his house in London. He was rich enough to buy Lord Albemarle's London house and endow it with one hundred thousand pounds in the name of the Davy-Faraday Laboratory. He might have had a peerage for the asking. But he turned again to his own laboratory and worked upon a process for obtaining the chlorine of ammonium chloride, by passing the vapour of ammonium chloride over nickel oxide. While introducing this gas into the vessel, Ludwig noticed its effect upon the nickel. They combined to form a gas, and Dr. Mond was faced with a phenomenon which all the accumulated scientific knowledge of the world could not explain to him.

Working with Dr. Langer, Mond burned the gas at the end of a glass pipe, to prevent it escaping into the room.

> One day, much to their astonishment, they found that this flame was burning an extraordinary green colour . . . when they held up a porcelain dish to cool the gas, they got a nickel mirror. Nobody had ever heard of a gas and metal forming a gaseous compound.

In a short record such as this I may not allow myself technical side-tracks. I want no more than to give this picture of Ludwig Mond, turning away from his success to work again. This time, through a sheer accident of the laboratory, he came upon the secret which led to the nickel process. This was so important that it became the inspiration of the company which has now become the International Nickel Company of Canada.

Ludwig Mond lived long enough to see his sons on the way to personal achievement. His second son had been swept into Westminster upon the Liberal tide of

1906. His eldest son was his companion in scientific experiment. There was little change in Dr. Mond, from the boy he had been in Cassel. He had pursued the line of his talents and the dictates of his character, never poisoned by meanness or vain ambition. His work is remembered more than his name.

In 1909 he confessed his age by the way he handed on the reins of control to his sons. He peered but dimly at the procession of figures bustling past him. I have written of the closing years of Ludwig Mond's life in my biography of his son. To paraphrase it now would be to make the picture self-conscious. The keen scientist had settled back comfortably into old age. His eyes were dim, so that he had to peer very closely at his beloved Titian, at " The Poplars." He sat like a patriarch in his chair, with two younger generations about him, bearing his name. The young approached him with fear and awe. He heard their laughter in the garden ; he heard them arriving in their stinking motor-cars. His century was passed, he said. He still went to Italy every winter and he gathered the friends in Rome about him. Now the collection of pictures in the palazzo was famous. He had already said that when he died they should be given to the National Gallery, so that *everybody* could enjoy them. Many of his friends were dead, and he had lived long enough to be lonely, among the last of his generation. The older workmen at Winnington, gnarled and tired, were dropping out one by one. Those who still lived were succoured on Ludwig's bounty. They too, the most humble of them, belonged to the grand veterans of industry now, and Ludwig honoured them. Now and again he went to Winnington. It had grown beyond his dreams . . . the dreams he had talked over with John Brunner in the 'sixties, when they found the calm park in which their great works were to be built. Now he was a shade in this enormous place, which was being extended and refreshed with new inventions. But his name was still exalted among his workers, even among the young ones, who had never seen him stamping through the works in his black coat and big hat. It is strange that even now, in 1933, one goes to Winnington and finds his name recalled with a curious sort of personal pride and pleasure. The stories have persisted, through all the rationalisation and changes since his time.

In the last days of his life, Winnington still looked upon him as master. The working men treasured tales of him : of his anger and his benevolence, his wrath and his tenderness. When he came back and peered close into their faces, searching here and there, with his dim eyes, for the ones he remembered ; when they heard his deep voice whisper, " I love to see old faces," their tongues were dry in their throats. His power was the awful power of character, and it intimidated them while it awakened their affections. There was something terrible about this mighty man, reduced to a huddled figure in a Bath chair. There were new directors and new chemists, with ideas as new-fangled as Ludwig Mond's ideas had been long ago. Still his name dominated them. Even when he was away, the memory of his power would excite their imagination. The stories of his fortitude, working day and night to realise his dream. The memory of his justice prevented them from bickering ; the consciousness that they were part of his great creation spurred them on to work for something more than their own material benefit. One story shone before them when they showed signs of discontent. In the early days, a disgruntled Irishman had approached Ludwig, suggesting that the men were dissatisfied. The man had been angry and unreasonable. " Take off

your coat and I'll fight you," was Ludwig's reply to
the insurgent. The men of Winnington did not forget
the story when contemplating Ludwig now, huddled
up in his chair. The dignity of history was coming to
the works and there was an older, more feeble generation sitting in the inns or about the cottage fires, talking
of the old days.

When Ludwig came for the last time, he was feeble
and quiet. They wheeled his chair up the road by
which he had walked with John Brunner almost forty
years before. They led him into the forest of towers
and overhead railways, great arches of steel and a
thousand windows, catching the sunlight. All was
owing to him. He paused in front of the Georgian
house in which he had lived. It seemed to be so
minute now, tucked in between the brick giants. He
still wore his big black hat and the long black coat
which they had all known. In the afternoon a thousand men gathered around him and he spoke to them.
Indeed, he was a patriarch. There was the silence
of deference, as they listened to him. He seemed to
grow, bigger and stronger, as they watched him. " I
have been ill—but I am better now. Very soon I shall
be working with you again."

One day, some months afterwards, Ludwig Mond's
grandson was called away from his class at school.
He was sent to London because, he was told, his grandfather was dying. The boy arrived at " The Poplars,"
and he was taken into the dark room where Ludwig
was resting, his tired eyes still shining above the long
white beard which made him seem so old and remote.
Outside the door were his older relations. They were
so still, so terrified in the knowledge that the great
man of their family was dying. He had ruled them
and he had showered money and kindness upon
them. He had taken their name from its humble

setting in Cassel and he had made it shine in exalted places.

Mrs. Mond led her son to the old man. Ludwig turned his white head until he could see the boy standing near to him. Mrs. Mond leaned over and said, " We all hope that Henry will carry on your tradition." The old man answered, " *We all hope* that Henry will make himself necessary."

His grandson was led out of the room and a few days afterwards Ludwig Mond died.

MARCEL PROUST
By Peter Quennell

MARCEL PROUST

MARCEL PROUST

By Peter Quennell

I

FEW writers, of any race or any period, have within so
short a time added so rich, so diverse, so densely popu-
lated a tract of intellectual territory to the imaginative
commonwealth of the Western hemisphere as did
Marcel Proust by the publication of his epic novel.
Its frontiers are conterminous with those of Europe :
it embraces the whole—at least, a very large section—
of urbanised, sophisticated modern life, and its personages, each of them typical yet individual, every one
of them drawn with extraordinary verve, have their
counterparts in most European cities. Talking of
Charlus, of Swann, of Madame Verdurin and " le
petit noyau," we find it difficult to speak of them as
of fictitious characters who enjoy no real life outside
the bulky fourteen-volume narrative through which
they originally made their appearance. For Proust's
reader they are social acquisitions whom, even though
he attempted to discard them, it would be impossible
to shake off. They have worked their way into the consciousness of the twentieth century as did Balzac's
characters into the fabric of the nineteenth ; the fact
that they are less romantic and more trivial—but then,
their triviality is very often truly tremendous—does
not reflect so much on the novelist as on his background.

Marcel Proust is sometimes judged by the life he
described. According to some critics—not always the
most penetrating—he was the cartographer, himself
decadent, of a decadent landscape, the anthropologist
who with a great deal of unnecessary care recorded the

tribal customs of the Cities of the Plain ; which, say
the critics, are best left undescribed.   Such criticism
is only applicable, if at all, to the later volumes of
Proust's enormous and extremely complex life-work ;
only in its closing chapters, where his stylistic and
creative power has begun to flag, do we recognise the
trace of spiritual malady and feel that he is obsessed
by, rather than legitimately interested in, the various
themes that it was his purpose to unfold. *A la
Recherche du Temps Perdu* is not a product of decadent
genius, for decadence implies limitations, a lack of
breadth and poise, both qualities without which so
long and absorbing a novel could never have existed.
The " humanity " for which critics are inclined to
bleat—as though " humanity " were in some way
consistent with " wholesomeness "—is implicit in the
very exuberance of the entire plan.

True, the human beings it introduces are odd
enough.   But are the human beings, with whom we
ourselves come into daily contact, any more "normal" ?
Is normality, in view of the attacks already delivered
by psychologists and psychiatrists, a myth jealously
maintained by abnormal people who attempt to super-
impose an air of everyday, commonsense decorum on
foundations which they know at bottom to be hopelessly and indecorously eccentric ?   The experiences
that give our lives value—that lend them their peculiar
tone and colour—are seldom experiences that would
find a place in the pages of an orthodox biography.
Manias, dreams, purely subjective occurrences for
which no form of words can be discovered, take an
important share in the construction of the least imaginative human minds.   Shadow and substance are
wildly confused ;   one of Proust's greatest assets as
a student of character was his refusal to allow the
substance, *qua* substance, a more important place in

his narrative scheme than those mere nothings that a
" sensible " man is inclined to dismiss. Caprice may
be as momentous as ambition, a vague velleity as influential as a reasoned desire ; since the novelist is
dealing with irrational creatures, whose wills are
swayed by something and by nothing, who dream
and plot and cogitate and brood, he cannot afford to
take up the line of superior reasonableness.

Intellectual prejudice must be put aside. There
is a touch of the teacher or preacher in almost every
nineteenth-century novelist and historian. Proust replaced the standpoint of the moralist by that of the
æsthete and by the calm dispassionate curiosity of the
modern scientific worker. Somewhat formidable, no
doubt, this habit of collecting and collating. Balzac
is often depicted in contemporary caricatures as a
Rabelaisian giant, surrounded by homunculi, either
stuck on pins or imprisoned in glass jars. But then
Balzac was a Romantic and a snob ; while Proust's
romanticism and snobbery were of a frigid, half-
mocking kind, always qualified by the inward smile
that one imagines must now and then have crossed
Disraeli's face, as with lavish Oriental gestures he
bowed himself out of the presence of his sovereign
mistress, Gloriana of Osborne and the Highlands.
Proust was never taken in by his own characters, as
was Balzac by some of the more highly-coloured fig-
ments of his teeming meridional brain ; his attitude,
for instance, towards the beautiful and high-born
duchesse de Guermantes, in whom he appreciated the
remembered charm of fields and villages near Combray
and the stored-up magnificence of French annals,
might be compared without undue exaggeration to
Disraeli's view of the royal personage, who was at
once Empress of India, the focus of literary day-dreams,
and a plain, limited, in many ways not at all intelligent

or fascinating Teutonic *Hausfrau*, at whose footstool he poured out his romantic dithyramb.

Disraeli gave England the Suez Canal ; just as important a gift to France in another sphere was the tract of territory—the line of intellectual communication—represented by Proust's gigantic book, the work of a writer who, though of French Catholic stock on his father's side, through his mother, born a Mlle Weil, came of a rich and cultured Jewish family. In race and temperament alike, Proust's mother and father belonged to different climates. No man could have been more energetic and single-minded than Professor Proust, the distinguished Inspector of Public Hygiene, while Madame Proust, who almost monopolised her son's affections, was sympathetic, retiring, and introspective. Two factors played a large part in the novelist's early development : his state of health—from the age of nine he had been subject to terrible asthmatic fits—and his relations with the mother he adored. At fourteen, against the printed question in a friend's album : *What is your idea of misery ?* he had written the significant sentence : " Être séparé de maman." Not until death robbed him of both parents—Madame Proust died, a widow, in 1905—did he make the crucial experiment of living alone.

Born in 1871, he spent the first thirty-four years of his life, if not beneath his mother's wing, at least under her roof, a young man whose strange habits and slipshod, unregulated hours—he rose late, only dressing to attend a party—were sanctified by the condition of his health. He was a dilettante and his passion was the world. Already, in 1896, when at the age of twenty-five he had published two little books, *Portraits de Peintres*, a handful of poems, accompanied by four piano-pieces by Reynaldo Hahn, and an elaborately illustrated and beautifully produced sheaf of essays in fiction, *Les Plaisirs et les Jours*, friends acquired at college had begun to murmur that the life Marcel Proust preferred to lead, and the acquaintances he ran after in the *grand monde*, were the ruin of a hopeful literary talent. Besides these two charming and gifted, but undoubtedly " slight," rather amateurish productions, he had translated a couple of Ruskin's books, *Sesame and the Lilies* and *The Bible of Amiens*; the study of French Gothic architecture, and the exploration of the Gothic labyrinths of the Faubourg Saint-Germain, were apparently the ruling motives of an idle existence.

Time was passing ; he was getting older and more infirm. Every occupation is, to some extent, a means of cheating—or attempting to escape from—the mordant unescapable sense of time ; our sense that the world is changing, that we ourselves are changing, that everything is transitory and that the flux of human life bears away upon its current all that we cling to—memories, affections, in the end even personality itself. Can literature prevail against the flood ? Is there anything that can be fixed, held down ; are there any values that do not change ? And, if such values there are, what is it that gives them their permanence ? These and other questions—questions that will occur more readily to an idle and self-indulgent than to an occupied and busily dutiful man—took shape at last in *A la Recherche du Temps Perdu*. The time that he had lost by dissipation, the days and months with their reveries, griefs, and pleasures that had slipped by him and plunged into the past, he was to draw up again towards the surface of his mind.

Yet, in the ordinary meaning of the word, Proust's novel is by no means autobiographical. His scheme demanded the presence of a narrator ; the narrator is himself ; the experience lived through is very largely his own experience ; but, since all experience is in the nature of things unsatisfactory, fugitive, and incomplete, it has been recombined, synthesised, distilled in the alembic of a literary imagination that added character to character, incident to incident, till it had obtained a purified and concentrated essence. Very definitely, the book is not a *roman à clef* ; no single person is portrayed, and, although it has been suggested that Madame Laure Heyman gave certain hints for the portrait of Odette de Crécy, that Robert de Saint-Loup includes a partial reflection of Proust's great friend, Bertrand de Fénelon, and that Swann is an amalgam of Charles Haas and Laforgue's patron, the Jewish art-collector, Ephrussi, it is equally clear that the relationship between these living personages and the personages in Proust's story is rather that of the metal or wooden supports, round which the clay model originally takes shape, and the statue as it leaves the sculptor's hands, than the relationship of the sitter and his painted effigy.

Time was the enemy, but it was also the ally, of Proust's genius. The period of sociability that seemed so futile had brought in a rich harvest of observations, stored away among the jumbled treasures of that astonishingly receptive brain, to be afterwards taken out, ticketed, classified, then incorporated, piece by piece, in the colossal structure. Friends had smiled at the eagerness with which " le petit Marcel " asked questions. What was the exact social standing, he would inquire, of this or that *grande dame* ? How would she behave in such and such circumstances ? How would she shake hands, how nod ? So exaggeratedly sensitive had he become to the vaguest and lightest shades of meaning, that his friendship—and he had many devoted friends—was now and then a source of deep embarrassment. Long, long letters flowed from his pen ; for every coldness, or lack of interest, that he thought he had noticed, for every *gaffe* or solecism of which he imagined he might have been guilty, he demanded, or lengthily furnished, an explanation. He combined the self-consciousness of a sensitive *parvenu* with the unself-conscious pertinacity of a born artist.

Yet, during those novice years, except for his trick of perpetually asking questions, the only evidence his friends received, of the great work all the while going forward, was his notebooks, in which he jotted down what then appeared to be disjointed character-sketches of men and women who had interested him, and the " imitations " he sometimes gave—pantomimic studies of Madeleine Lemaire, the fashionable illustrator, who kept a much-frequented Bohemian *salon*, bidding her guests good-bye, or of Robert de Montesquiou, that literary *gentilhomme*, some of whose mannerisms were transferred to Charlus, displaying his emblazoned peacock's tail. Proust had a wonderfully capacious memory ; after a short expedition to Venice with his mother and Reynaldo Hahn, undertaken before his father's death in 1903, he never again left France and, indeed, very seldom left Paris. The summer he would spend at Trouville or at Cabourg, a Norman seaside resort that lent brilliance to his enchanting description of Balbec ; while during the autumn, winter, and spring he lived immured in his mother's flat, his habits, as his asthma grew worse and worse, growing steadily more and more nocturnal, till they had reached a point at which he rarely got up during the daytime and was visited by, or telephoned to, his friends usually at midnight, or at one and two o'clock in the morning.

Memory was then almost his sole resource. Soon after 1905, when he lost his mother, he began a gradual but definite retirement from the world, interrupted only by brief excursions. In the dusty solitude of his bedchamber above the Boulevard Haussmann, that strange, shuttered, airless, cork-lined room, thick with the smoke of fumigations, littered with fallen sheets of paper, much encumbered by the presence of a huge grand piano and lighted very dimly by a hanging lamp, the hermit, wearing gloves, swaddled in a cocoon of woollen waistcoats, had started off—though he scarcely left his bed—on his journey down the perspective of the years. " Longtemps, je me suis couché de bonne heure " goes the first sentence of the first paragraph of *Du Côté de Chez Swann*, and, through pages of delicate analysis, he records his sensations when falling asleep, in the end carrying us back to Combray, the small French provincial town in which he was brought up, and the nervous terrors and agitations which then, for an over-sensitive and invalidish little boy, attended the moment of seeking his bed.

Recollections of childhood, of his mother and grandmother, and of M. Swann, who lived not far away and was reputed to have made a shameful marriage, occupy the greater part of the first volume. *Un Amour de Swann*, the story of Swann's love affair with Odette de Crécy, has on the face of it a somewhat remote connection with the first and third episodes between which it is printed, since it is already ancient history, leads us from Combray to Paris, and introduces an entirely new set of characters. Although the element of time is so important in the scheme of *A la Recherche du Temps Perdu*, chronological accuracy is not preserved. As in the pattern of a fugue, the time *motif* appears and disappears, threatens, evaporates, or seems to impend ; it pervades the narrative, but does not control or restrict its leisurely movement, which develops, as memory develops, at the smallest provocation. Since time is implicit in the whole subject, Proust did not feel the need of a definite chronological framework.

Time flows on, a stream full of eddies and back-currents, and, like a kingfisher, the narrator's imagination glances obliquely to and fro across its broad, discoloured expanse, lighting up now Combray and his parent's house, now Paris and the *salon* of the Verdurins, now the romantic dusk of Odette's drawing-room.

We do not ourselves come to maturity in any regular or systematic fashion. We grow, as Proust's novel grows, by fits and starts, in sudden and unexpected leaps. Or, perhaps, it might be more accurate to say that, although we are continually changing, we are only aware of the changes that have overtaken us in flashes of rare illumination. The rushing sound of Time's chariot is always in our ears ; we know—to use Jean Cocteau's image—that we are passengers on an express train hurrying us at full speed towards death, but although the same pace is pitilessly maintained, we are aware of it at different stages in different degrees ; for we have, so to speak, our own interior pace and rhythm, now slower and now faster, a rhythm beneath and through which, as we realise ever and again with appalling distinctness, runs the deep mechanical rub-a-dub of passing time.

Yet moments, after all, do occur that we are tempted to describe as " timeless." Suddenly, not for long, our sense of time ceases to function and we recapture, just as if the train had come to a standstill or had mysteriously wheeled upon its tracks, a glimpse of some landscape left behind many years ago. Such is the dominant theme of Proust's two concluding volumes, *Le Temps Retrouvé*. The narrator emerges from isolation to find his friends so changed during his absence that they are many of them barely recognisable; but he makes another discovery—that a mere physical accident, such as stumbling on a paving-stone lower than its fellows (an accident that had already occurred to him in the Baptistery of Saint Mark's at Venice) may recall, more fresh and vivid than the day he first enjoyed them, sensations that he grasps as perhaps the only form of reality worth experiencing, since they, at least—these still virgin fragments recovered from the flood of time—have neither faded nor changed.

In one aspect, then, the purpose of *A la Recherche du Temps Perdu* is the discovery and literary analysis of sensations that have defied the work of time. Past, present, future, writes the novelist, may be equally arid ;

> but should a sound, should a scent, heard and breathed long ago, be heard and breathed again, at once in the present and in the past, real without being actual, ideal without being abstract, then immediately the essence of things, permanent but for the most part hidden, is liberated and our true self, which may have seemed extinct for many years . . . wakes and quickens as it receives the celestial offering.

This true self the narrator hopes to regain. He is in search of times gone by, because there and there alone can he hope to recover the " deathless " or " timeless " part of his own existence. His search assumes the proportions of a mystical quest which leads him back through the submarine labyrinths of a vanished world.

II

Characteristically enough, it is the conclusion of *A la Recherche du Temps Perdu* that indicates its starting-point. I have attempted, very briefly, to describe the nature of the expedition ; and it now remains to say something of its course, particularly as it traversed the landscape of modern society. Proust, we are told, was a snob and a *parvenu* ; more than a hundred closely printed pages are devoted, in the second volume of *Le Côté de Guermantes*, to an evocation of the duchesse de Guermantes' dinner-party, which is chronicled by the narrator with a minuteness usually reserved for diplomatic conferences and momentous political crises. Nothing happens ; but then the things that happen, as political history teaches us, have generally an importance in inverse ratio to the noise they stir up and the clamour with which they are saluted. No, nothing happens ; the duchesse de Guermantes dutifully shows off her wit before that admiring, incredulous, semi-royal ninny, the princesse de Parme, while her husband acts as ring-master, calls attention to his wife's sallies and underlines, with bland complacency, her more brilliant flights. The three portraits thus created are unforgettable ; an impatient satirist might have dismissed this congregation of well-fed, highly born, congenitally stupid human beings with a smile or an angry shrug of the shoulders. Proust's satire lies curled up like an Egyptian asp—it is sufficiently venomous to annihilate the entire Faubourg—in a bright bouquet of romantic adulation.

How fascinating were *les gens du monde* and, heavens, how foolish ! It is to be doubted whether a young man, whose constitution did not include a strain of typically Jewish romanticism, would have troubled to worm his way quite so patiently, quite so dextrously, into the archaic universe of the pre-war Faubourg Saint-Germain, or whether, having penetrated, he would have retained quite the same degree of mocking independence. The position of a Jew in Western Europe is often much less rigid, less pre-established by birth and tradition, and the traditional sentiments they are inclined to produce, than that of his Gentile brethren. If he is rich, talented, and agreeable, he may " go far "—as far as Charles Haas, Swann, or

Proust himself. Like them, he may make friends in
the aristocracy ; but, to whatever society he adapts his
gifts, he is *in* it, rather than *of* it, an adventurer always
somewhat apart, who, though he admires or adores,
since he is very often more intelligent than his Christian
contemporaries, cannot refrain now and then from a
malicious smile.

I do not wish to over-emphasise the distinctively
Jewish strain in Proust's temperament, but it may be
as well to sum up here some of his more obvious racial
traits. I have cited the combination of romantic
snobbery and critical independence, also found in no
less a Jew than Lord Beaconsfield ; and one must add
the faculty of assimilating, and getting the best from,
the characteristics of the nation among whom their
tents are pitched, that many Jews have carried to a
fine art. Proust, of course, was half French, and the
half of him that was not French seems but to have
made him more French still. No nationalist, in the
aggressive sense of the word, he was deeply and
romantically patriotic, with a passion for French history, the names of French towns and villages, the
architecture of French cathedrals, and the rustic
patois that he heard on a servant's lips. Of such
details, some of his most delightful passages are composed ; Françoise, the grumbling, cantankerous *bonne*,
is a representative of the French peasantry, and he is
enchanted, in the language she employs, to detect
many turns of speech used by the duchesse de Guermantes. He approaches his aristocrats, not as a poly-
glot, enfranchised snob, but as a profound and learned
student of Saint-Simon.

Last of all, his extraordinarily acute sensitiveness.
Jews have often been credited with a kind of emotional
masochism that takes the form of a desire to be flouted
or abused by the persons they most affect. In *La*

Prisonnière and *Albertine Disparue*, his account of the
extravagances of jealous misery to which the narrator
so readily, almost greedily, abandons himself, tem-
porarily wrecks the balance of Proust's scheme. The
agonised divagations of the wretched lover are pitched
in a key as intense and fatiguing as the lamentations of
Jeremiah or Job. Suppose, we grumble, that Albertine *has* gone—she was not irreplaceable or unique. . . .
But, at this point, we are brought up against Proust's
individual and highly poetic philosophy of love. I
have suggested elsewhere that the romanticism of *A
la Recherche du Temps Perdu* bears a close resemblance
to the romantic attitude of the author of *Sylvie* and
Le Rêve et la Vie, since both writers " make a novel
distinction between the object and the response it
stirs." While the true Romantic pretended to identify
object and passion—the quality of the woman and the
quality of the love she aroused—both Proust and
Gérard de Nerval were concerned to isolate that
passion, to show it vibrating in the void, to hear its
musical reverberations dying away. " La femme
réelle," Gérard wrote, describing the generation among
which he attained to manhood, " révoltait notre in-
génuité." Similarly, Proust, with his very marked
homosexual interests and the natural elusiveness that
characterised everything he did, though his protagonists desire and possess a large variety of women,
lifts his account of these adventures on to a plane
where the physical transaction itself becomes relatively
unimportant. Indeed, there is an ambiguity surround-
ing the figure of Albertine, who appears at moments
to be less girl than boy, a hint of perversity or impotence underlying the temperament of her lover, an
air of mystery enshrouding the entire relationship, that
persuades a reader—as Proust, no doubt, intended that
it should—to devote his whole attention to its poetic,

or subjective, aspect. Proust's method is to exalt the attraction itself at the expense of the human personality round which it centres. He spares no pains to break up such attractions into their poetic, romantic, or allegorical constituents, explaining how his early infatuation for the duchesse de Guermantes was inseparable from the historic glamour of her blazon and the territorial associations of her name ; how Albertine evoked Balbec and the background of sea and sky against which he had first seen her move ; how Swann, in Odette de Crécy, a pretentious and slightly faded *demi-mondaine*, had seen the Jethro's daughter of a fresco in the Sistine Chapel, narrating therewith the long process of entanglement which had led to his making her his wife. Entanglements of that kind— entanglements into which a lover only sinks the more hopelessly, as he imagines that he is directing his steps towards dry land—have never been depicted with greater exactitude. " What *can* he have seen in her ? " —that familiar query—is proposed in all its anguish and resolved in all its myriad complications.

His sort [writes Proust, of Swann and Odette] in point of fact . . . she had never been, and yet she had been the object of his deep and painful love. Later, he was himself surprised by this contradiction ; but, after all, there need be no contradiction if we reflect how pronounced in the lives of most men is the proportion of suffering caused by women who were " not their sort." It may be traced, perhaps, to a large number of causes. Because they are not your sort, you begin by allowing yourself to be loved without loving in return, hence falling under the domination of a habit that would never have come to pass with a woman who, being your sort and realising your need of her, would not have made herself cheap, would have permitted relatively few meetings and would never have assumed that intimate connection with every hour of our day which has the subsequent

effect, should our mistress chance to fail us . . . of breaking
not one bond of sympathy but a thousand. And then this
habit is sentimental, because it is based upon no very urgent
physical desire and, if love is born, the brain becomes proportionately busy. . . . A woman of our own sort is seldom
dangerous, for she has no ulterior motive, satisfies, soon
leaves us, does not install herself in our day-to-day existence ;
and what is dangerous and causes suffering in love is not the
woman herself ; it is her presence every day ; our curiosity
to know what she is doing at any given moment ; it is not
the woman, so much as habit.

This knack of extracting from human beings a poetic
or symbolical significance that transcends and obscures
their human personality, Proust did not confine to his
analysis of love. His aptitude for arranging his characters in some symbolical, even mythological, pattern
seems, now and then, too elaborately developed, his
vision unnecessarily comprehensive. He saw everything, every detail, all at once. Society appeared
before his eyes like a mammoth Hindu edifice, one of
those towering pyramidal structures, where every
coign, every ledge, is thickly peopled with astonishing
and grotesque symbolism. He must throw his outline
around the whole ; he must weave his scrutiny among
the crabbedest fretwork of its balustrades. Not content with literary impressionism, he determined to
reproduce the entire fabric ; and it was thus, with the
reckless disregard of a man in whom inspiration had
become illumination, that he would permit his
parentheses to hurry on till they had brimmed the
page and were pouring, rapid and intricate, down the
next ; that he wrote often clumsily, sometimes hide-
ously. . . . Here a naturalist might have failed,
tumbling suffocated beneath the tremendous weight
of his material. That Proust, by temperament, was so
little of a naturalist, had after all, so slight a regard for

realism, proved the ultimate salvation of his book. He had none of that reverence for raw fact, that pathetic reliance on observed phenomena, which had been the undoing of Zola and the Goncourts and is curiously echoed to-day in the work of Mr. James Joyce, an old-fashioned realist, roughly turned inside out. Like the Goncourts, he was an inveterate observer ; he belonged to the tribe of literary scientists, but his observations were always subsidiary. Not a fact, not a personal or social peculiarity did he unearth, but, in cleansing and burnishing it, he gave it the colour of his own mind.

No writer is apparently more diffuse ; few are actually more consistent. His method of preparing for the entrance of a new character by allowing us, as it were, first of all to see the character's shadow projected from behind the scenes and hear his or her voice off, has been likened to that of the great Japanese woman novelist, Lady Murasaki. Proust seldom mislays a character ; even " la femme de chambre de Madame Putbus," who never appears but whose mercenary favours the narrator had once planned to enjoy, is referred to again and again in a comic undertone. During *Le Côté de Guermantes* and the three volumes of *Sodome et Gomorrhe*, figure after figure presses forward on to the already crowded stage. Artistically, the effect of *La Prisonnière* and *Albertine Disparue* is disappointing. The stage is cleared ; all the interest of the narrative is concentrated on a meticulous, brilliant yet rather wearisome exploration of the origin and results of sexual jealousy. The narrator becomes more and more self-centred, his maunderings progressively more ignominious, till the most tolerant reader's patience is put to flight.

Proust did not live to see the publication of these concluding, and in many ways inferior, volumes. *Du Côté de Chez Swann*, printed in 1913, after a struggle

with timid and recalcitrant publishers which had
lasted two whole years, found its circle of admirers
very gradually during the war. *A l'Ombre des Jeunes
Filles en Fleurs*, ready by 1914, was not published till
after the Armistice, when, in spite of bitter opposition,
it was awarded the Prix Goncourt. Proust, whom his
early critics had brushed aside as a mere *boulevardier*—
André Gide, who subsequently announced that he
tasted in its style " a lake of delights," had refused
Du Côté de Chez Swann on behalf of the *Nouvelle
Revue Française*—was now at length famous. He
had secured the recognition of his great achievement ;
he had three years longer to live in the world.

To its pleasures and distractions he was already
dead. As a *revenant*, it is true, he would sometimes
return to his old haunts ; one night, for instance, he
had risen, dressed himself and struggled out to a
fashionable party, where he wished to observe just
how the prince de Sagan wore his monocle. To the
end, he often visited the Ritz, dining alone in a private
room or downstairs among the other guests, from
whom he was distinguished by the heavy fur-lined
overcoat that never left his shoulders, by his white
face and huge violet-circled eyes. With the waiters
and *maître d'hôtel* he carried on an incessant and
animated conversation, questioning them as eagerly
about their habits and personal pursuits as he did the
duchess whom he questioned about the hats and
dresses she had worn twenty years ago. His rather
hysterical generosity still assumed the form of huge
and unexpected tips which he dispensed, not so much
from a love of display, as from an exaggerated and
hyperbolical sensitiveness to the imagined feelings of
others. Rather than offend or disappoint a single
man, he would take the precaution of tipping every
waiter in a restaurant. " That waiter in the corner,"

he would remark pensively, " has not yet had anything from us," and, when his friends protested that
the man had not served at their table—" But haven't
you noticed how wretched he looks ? . . . "   And the
waiter would be summoned to receive fifty or a hundred
francs.

At home, he inhabited the cell of a literary anchorite.
Proofs were corrected and recorrected ; great streamers
of additional matter were inserted in the printed text,
and sheet upon sheet of voluminous after-thoughts
pinned, gummed, or cobbled to the written page.   For
many years, he had used narcotic or stimulant drugs ;
and, having drowsed for three days under the influence
of veronal, he would keep himself awake for the three
succeeding days with the help of repeated doses of
caffein.   The journeys in a closed car, that he had
occasionally made to see the blossoms of the Norman
apple-orchards, had long been abandoned.   He loved
flowers ; and now the chestnut blooms of the Boulevard Haussmann under his window were themselves
only visited in imagination.   He remembered, his
friends described them ; and that was enough.   A
grain of pollen, a drop of scent upon a handkerchief,
would produce one of those terrible asthmatic crises,
only to be kept at bay by shuttered and hermetically
sealed casements, by fumigating himself and his room
with dense clouds of smoke, behind which, drawn up
uncomfortably in bed, wrapped in thick layers of wool
and flannel, he suggested some half-mummified
mediæval alchemist.   Doctors, as the end approached,
he refused to see.   During the summer of 1922, he
caught cold, and the cold brought on a series of complications, which finally precipitated an attack of
pneumonia.   He expired on November 18, still lucid,
although suffering great pain.

Seldom has a literary martyrdom been more complete. During the night that preceded his death, he was busy dictating an addition to the splendid passage in which he had described the last days of Bergotte, the novelist, using his own symptoms as material. Ringed and splashed by the spilth of glasses and medicine-bottles, near his bed was found a scrap of paper bearing, among much that was illegibly scrawled, the name of M. de Forcheville, Odette's second husband and one of the original and most unpleasant members of " le petit noyau," as it is described in *Un Amour de Swann*. He had died, with the courage and obstinacy of his race, amid thoughts of the work that had become more important to himself and to the world at large than the life on which it battened. Genius is usually a kind of parasite ; microscopic and unprotected when it first enters a human organism, it may develop—in Proust's case, it did develop—till it has engrossed every function of body and mind. All that it leaves of its victim is a walking wraith, or a husky voice in the dim recesses of a cork-lined room.

Several years after Proust's death, the publication of *Le Temps Retrouvé* brought his work to a close. The culminating passage, one of the finest he ever constructed, is also one of the most important if we are to understand his book in the spirit in which it was written. Proust's system has an affinity, perhaps not wholly deceptive, with that of Einstein. Like the modern physicist, Proust makes time his fourth dimension ; he, too, has disrupted the Euclidean three-dimensional universe—in literature corresponding to the practice of realism—by the new and disturbing element he has introduced. " An individual," observes Eddington, " is a four-dimensional object of greatly elongated form ; in ordinary language we say that he has considerable extension in time and insignificant extension in space."

Now turn to the ultimate paragraphs of *Le Temps Retrouvé* :

I experienced [writes Proust] a sensation of profound weariness when I reflected that this enormous extent of time had not only been lived, thought, secreted without interruption by me, that it was my life, that it was myself, but that at every moment of the day I had to carry it along with me, that it supported me, that I was perched upon its dizzy apex and that I could never move without displacing it too. . . . I understood now why it was that the duc de Guermantes, whom I had been surprised to find, when I saw him sitting on a chair, so little aged, though the years beneath him were so much more numerous than mine, had, when he rose and tried to hold himself upright, wavered on legs as unstable as the legs of one of those venerable archbishops about whom nothing is solid except their metal cross . . . just as if human beings were hoisted upon living stilts which grew steadily longer and longer, loftier sometimes than the tallest belfry . . . from which all of a sudden they tumble headlong. I trembled to think how tall underfoot were mine already ; I felt that I should not have the strength to carry with me much further this past already so extensive, which I carried so painfully in myself ! Yet should, after all, sufficient leisure be allowed me to accomplish my work, I would not fail to mark it with the seal of Time, of which the conception had been so forcibly impressed upon me to-day ; I would describe human beings, even though it were at the cost of making them appear monsters, as the occupants in Time of a position very different from the position they occupy in space, a position boundlessly extended, since, like giants plumbing the years, they touch at one and the same instant periods utterly remote—with a great gulf of days flowing between—in Time.

These sentences are Proust's last words ; they are the apology and vindication of his tremendous effort. Notice, by the way, how significant is the interval that separates Proust from the attitude of his nineteenth-century predecessors. Where now is the sense of human dignity that, for its own sake, made a man's tragic or commonplace life-history worth telling? Human beings and their passions have only a subjective, or relative, importance. Man has no destiny save to extract from the hurly-burly of his sensations their quintessential, or " timeless," element, for in the flux of changing and dream-like phenomena, this alone, Proust announces, is real and unchanging. Instead of the doctrine of perfectibility—the view of Man as a progressive, ambitious animal—we find a recognition of his poetic and symbolic value.

WALTHER RATHENAU
By C. R. S. HARRIS

WALTHER RATHENAU

WALTHER RATHENAU

By C. R. S. HARRIS

IT is curious to reflect how many Jews have been
massacred and how few have been assassinated. The
distinction between these two forms of murder is not
quite so trivial as might at first sight be supposed, for
it provides a key to one of the more striking characteristics of the Jewish race—that marked aversion
to public life in all its forms, which even in this
country is still, with some notable exceptions, dis-
cernible. That aversion can, of course, be explained
easily enough on historical grounds, especially in Central Europe. But the fact remains that all the world
over the Jews still tend to form a community apart,
an alien element which neither persecution nor the
most generous equality of treatment has enabled the
national organism wholly to assimilate. To this
general rule Walther Rathenau was a conspicuous
exception. For though by a grim irony of fate he
succumbed to the assassin's bullet, as a victim of that
barbarous and revolting anti-Semitism which seems
to be endemic among the German people, he was, in
fact, a fervent admirer of Prussianism and a convinced
patriot, one of whose earliest ideals was the complete
Germanisation of the children of Abraham within the
national frontiers. Yet for all his convictions no man
can wholly escape from his ancestral inheritance, and
the struggle between the Prussian and the Jew was
largely, as we shall see, to determine his tragic destiny.

Indeed, this conflict seemed almost to be fore-
shadowed by the accidental conjunction of his nativity.
He was born in Berlin, on September 29, 1867, the eve
of the great Jewish festival of the New Year, which on

that occasion coincided with the feast of St. Michael, the Angelic patron and defender of Christian Germany. His father, Emil Rathenau, who was afterwards to become the founder of the world-famous A.E.G., was at that time an obscure Jewish ironmaster, who had married into a rich and cultured family of Frankfurt bankers. Emil Rathenau, the Ford of the nineteenth century, was a typical case of the " one-track " mind, to which all literary and artistic activities were a closed book. But he possessed an amazing constructive genius for industrial organisation and applied science. He was the first European to recognise the practical importance of Edison's electrical inventions, and by a brilliant stroke of business bought up his patents and thus laid the foundations of the German electrical industry. In close co-operation with the banks he built up the great horizontal trust which finally developed into the German General Electric Company (A.E.G.). He was thus one of the principal pioneers of what is now called rationalisation, i.e. mass-production and large-scale combinations—ideas which were to exercise an all-important influence on the growth of German industry. Mathilde Rathenau, Walther's mother, was a very different character. She was a highly gifted woman, much given to literature and the arts, especially music, quick and clever, with a lively imagination and an intuitive understanding of human beings, firm and dignified though somewhat sentimental.

It is always tempting to analyse a complex personality into its hereditary elements, and Walther Rathenau affords unusual scope for such an interesting exercise. For he seems to have inherited in a supreme degree practically all the capacities of both his parents. On the paternal character of the shrewd business man, the master of applied science, the organiser of a world-wide industrial concern, he superimposed the entirely

different nature of his mother, from whom he inherited his strongly idealistic, slightly sentimental
strain, his extraordinary sensitiveness to beauty in
all its forms, and, above all, his fertile and delicate
imagination. The fusion of these diverse elements,
developed by careful self-discipline and assiduous
training, gave him an extraordinary versatility, a many-
sidedness of intellect which was truly an astonishing
phenomenon. Yet the fusion was never quite complete. As his friend Reicke once remarked, " Walther
Rathenau has the head of a business man and the
heart of a lyric poet," and the head and the heart
were continually at war, in spite of a lifelong effort
to reconcile them. This internal struggle was hidden,
except to a few intimate friends, beneath a cold and
slightly distant exterior, and the effort to overcome it
was masked by a carefully cultivated self-consciousness
which was interpreted by his enemies, not wholly un-
justly, as inordinate vanity.

But the conflict between the poet and the business
man was only one aspect of an even deeper struggle,
the conflict between the Prussian and the Jew. In
early manhood the distinction between the two was
branded on his soul by a bitter experience. Brought
up like all good Prussian schoolboys to regard the
Army as the only honourable profession, he found,
on doing his military service in the Horse Guards, that
the road to a Commission was barred by the fact that he
was a Jew, and suddenly he realised that he belonged to
an inferior race.

> In the life of every German Jew there comes a moment
> which he remembers with pain as long as he lives ; when
> he becomes for the first time fully conscious of the fact that
> he has entered the world as a citizen of the second class
> and that no amount of ability or merit can rid him of this
> status.

This discovery, which might have poisoned a less generous spirit, profoundly affected his whole outlook, but in a rather unexpected way. Instead of arousing in him an intellectual disdain or hatred for the dominant caste, it only intensified his passionate admiration for the Nordic nobility with its instinctive sense of values and its aristocratic, unself-conscious acceptance of life, so different from his own complicated nature. But the Jewish intelligence could never be wholly dominated by the Prussian spirit, and the half-conscious realisation of their incompatibility, while at times it showed itself in outspoken criticism of the short-comings of the ruling class, served only to reinforce his profound depreciation of the intellect. Yet by a curious paradox, it was precisely through the development of the intellectual faculties that he unconsciously sought compensation for the ignoble accident of his birth. This desire to excel and to surpass others with the superiority of his intellectual achievements, a typically Jewish trait very noticeable, for example, in the young Disraeli, will probably be explained in the fashionable jargon of to-day as proceeding from an inferiority complex which was at the same time the source of that distinction between the fear-man (Jew) and the man of courage (Prussian) upon which he was prone to lay so much stress—a distinction which he also symbolised by his sharp differentiation between the purposive intellect and the soul. Hence, too, the fundamental weakness of his personality, a certain over-refinement of the intelligence which inhibited the development of his emotions and by its self-generated distrust sterilised its own creative powers. And so Rathenau, for all his remarkable gifts and notable achievements, missed the highest eminence as if by a hand's-breadth, both in the theoretical and the practical sphere. Yet his achievements in both were sufficiently striking to mark him out as perhaps the most distinguished of the secondary personages of our age.

In obedience to his father's wish, Rathenau, who had been tempted to become a painter, like his father's kinsman, Max Liebermann, rather reluctantly went into industry, after taking his Doctor's degree in Natural Science. His first post was at Neuhausen, in Switzerland, where he worked in an electro-chemical factory belonging to a subsidiary of his father's concern on a process for obtaining chlorine by electrolysis. Two years later he erected the first electro-chemical works in Germany at Bitterfeld, which he managed for seven years. As a technician he seems to have had remarkable success ; he patented several electrolytical processes for obtaining ferrosilicon, chromium, magnesium, etc., and superintended the erection of further electrochemical plants in France and Poland. In 1899 he was co-opted to the Board of the A.E.G., and for three years took over the construction of powerstations, building a number of them in foreign countries, e.g. in Manchester, Amsterdam, Buenos Ayres, Baku. In 1902 he left his father's firm to enter the Berliner Handelsgesellschaft, a bank of the peculiar German type, largely interested in the financing of industrial undertakings.

Rathenau thus abandoned the technical sphere of industry after a comparatively short career, but not before he had already made his mark. For it has been reported that Hugo Stinnes, the great industrial magnate of the post-war period (who, incidentally, detested him), once described him as Germany's greatest industrial genius in the technical field. But it was rather in the twin spheres of finance and organisation that he really became famous. Half industrialist and half banker—a hybrid type which Germany bred with such conspicuous success—he came on the scene just at the time when in Germany, and elsewhere on the Continent, industry was rapidly transforming itself by a process of integration and fusion into large-scale units. As representative of the Berliner Handelsgesellschaft and of the A.E.G. (for he retained his seat on the Board), he was responsible for the reorganisation of a large number of undertakings, covering a great diversity of industries, and his activities stretched far beyond the frontiers of the German Reich. Directorship after directorship flowed in upon him, and the list of the undertakings in which he was interested, given by Count Harry Kessler in his admirable biography, is astonishing. In the ten years which preceded the war Rathenau played a leading part in the direction of no less than eighty-six German and twenty-one foreign enterprises : in Italy, Switzerland, South America, Spain, Africa, Finland, France, Austria, and Russia. His interests were spread almost over the entire field of German industry, including, besides electricity, the metal industries, mining, railways, chemicals, telegraphs and cables, banks and trust companies, textiles, aviation, glass, potash, carriage and wagon building, motor-cars, paper-making, and pottery. This almost incredible range of activities gave him a unique insight into the financial and industrial structure of Continental Europe, which proved of momentous importance to Germany during the war, for it equipped him as no other man could have been equipped for the gigantic task of organising the supplies of raw materials in a blockaded country.

But these activities, far from exhausting it, expressed only one aspect of his many-sided personality. For besides being one of the foremost captains of industry, he was a conspicuous example of that universal cultivation which since the Renaissance had seemed almost lost. Though he was by no means academically inclined, all learning was, in a sense, his province. He spoke English, French, and Italian almost as perfectly as his own native tongue. He was conversant with the whole field of European literature, as well as with the more recent developments of the arts and the sciences. There was no topic of general interest, from horse-racing to molecular physics, from French art to engineering, with which he did not seem perfectly familiar, and when he met an expert in no matter what subject, he appeared to be able to converse with him with perfect ease in the language of his own faculty. In fact, he was the living embodiment of a sort of pentecostal miracle. In addition, he could paint a picture or play a Beethoven sonata in a manner which would do credit to the most gifted amateur, and he was, also, something of a poet. But it was as a philosophical critic of the modern age and as a champion of the spiritual life that he took himself most seriously. During a voyage to Greece in the early years of the present century, Rathenau discovered the soul, and the discovery profoundly changed his whole outlook upon life. For though his activities as a practical man of business were in no way diminished, they began to assume in his own estimation of himself a much less important perspective, and it was as the precursor of a new social era, half-prophet and half-statesman, that he was worshipped by his admirers and derided by his enemies.

This astounding versatility of intellectual endowment was combined with a slightly sentimental, over-refined, romantic idealism, which threw a haze of good-will over the inconsistencies and impracticabilities of his social schemes. For Rathenau thought in pictures rather than in syllogisms, he detested argument and despised the careful discipline of academic ratiocination, which he regarded as stale and lifeless. Moreover, the highly self-conscious cultivation of these intellectual and spiritual faculties was marred by a certain lack of virility which sometimes bordered on the morbid, an absence of robustness which rendered him touchy and over-sensitive. This defect exercised a peculiarly disastrous effect on his personal relations which were characterised by a baffling alternation of icy reserve and wistful sentimentalism, of morbid suspicion of the friendly overtures of his fellow-creatures, and a pathetic demand for human sympathy. The result was a quick succession of brief and almost passionate friendships, and a growing list of enemies. Not that the social side of his nature was defective or that he lacked social gifts. Tall and distinguished-looking, he had made his début in German society, in spite of his Jewish birth which he never attempted to conceal, with conspicuous success. He frequented the salons of the most brilliant hostesses of the day, like Princess von Bülow and the fascinating Frau von Hindenburg. Without being in the least snobbish, he obviously enjoyed Society, and his perfectly dressed figure was, for a time at any rate, frequently to be seen in Court circles, where he enjoyed the acquaintance, if not the friendship, of the Kaiser. He was on intimate terms too with most of the best-known artists, musicians, and men of letters of the day. Yet in spite of a very great variety of social connections he was a singularly lonely man, and the only love affair which is known to have stirred his rather frigid passions was destined to be little more than a romantic dream. In his personal habits he cultivated a severe, almost puritan, discipline, albeit tempered with a somewhat luxurious æstheticism. Indeed, both in his villa in the Grünewald and in the small but exquisite Royal Castle of Freienwalde, in which he took such immense pride, he lived amid exquisite surroundings a life of expensive and elegant simplicity.

It is not at all surprising that his contemporaries
should have found him difficult to understand, for he
was not one person, but a host of persons synthetised
into a single consciousness. If we can imagine, for
example, Alfred Mond amalgamated with Arthur
Balfour, and flavoured with a dash of Ruskin, a flavour
of Carlyle, a spot of Pater, a strong dose of Professor
Gilbert Murray, and more than a suspicion of Mr.
H. G. Wells, we may perhaps get something of the
interesting complexity of his character. There was,
moreover, something about him which was just slightly
exaggerated ; a rarefied kind of vanity which exposed
him to a certain amount of satire, in spite of the
superiority of his attainments and the undeniable
nobility of his character. Thus, for example, Robert
Musil's very unkind portrait of him under the name
of Dr. Arnheim, in *Der Mann ohne Eigenschaften*, in
spite of its obvious malice, carries with it an uncom-
fortable degree of conviction.

In almost any other European country except Germany, such a multiplicity of talents would have
destined their possessor for a political career. But
Rathenau was born a Jew, and Jews were automatically
excluded, not from Parliamentary politics, but from
the official hierarchy. It is true that by judicious
baptism this barrier might have been overcome. But
Rathenau, though he was *anima naturaliter Christiana*,
was, unlike Henry of Navarre, too upright for a
political conversion. And the Parliamentary career,
though he was on one occasion tempted by it, offered
little scope for his ambition. For the Reichstag was
little more than a " talking shop " ; the real power lay,
not with the Parliamentarians, but with the official
caste, the Junker oligarchy, from which the officers of
the three services were drawn. Of that oligarchy
Rathenau was a critical but sincere admirer. It

embodied his ideal of the *Mutmensch*, the instinctive
Nordic superman, but its horizon was altogether too
limited to win his unqualified approval. With increasing clearness, as the first decade of the century
went by the defects of the whole structure impressed
themselves upon him, the blind and narrow arrogance
of the landed aristocracy, the materialistic servility of
the rich bourgeoisie, the pathetic helplessness of the
working classes and, above all, the reckless irresponsi-
bility of William II and his entourage. Hence, in
spite of a certain aristocratic bias in his nature, he came
to identify himself more and more with those who
were in favour of a constitutional monarchy on the
English democratic model, with a ministry responsible,
not to the Kaiser in person, but to Parliament. Not
that he was particularly wedded to democratic forms ;
what impressed him most was the need for leadership
and the fact that the ruling caste was no longer com-
petent to govern a nation of sixty-five million souls.
He saw, too, clearly enough where the " big-Navy "
policy of von Bülow and the vanity of the Kaiser were
leading. All through those last fateful years, while
Germany was piling up her land armaments and building her colossal navy, Rathenau was preaching, not
peace as such, for he was no pacifist, but the profounder
doctrine that the real power of a nation does not consist
in weapons of war or ingots of steel, but in the moral
and spiritual forces of its citizens. He recognised,
too, what von Bülow, for all his diplomatic experience,
never clearly grasped, that the building of the German
fleet was inevitably antagonising British public opinion,
and more than once he made suggestions, albeit not
very practical ones, for a quota system to stop the
race in shipbuilding, and during those last few hectic
days, when Europe was plunging frantically over the
abyss, he protested loudly against the manner in which

German policy was being dragged helplessly behind the wheels of the Austrian chariot. Yet when the final hour struck his loyalty did not falter, and by a singular irony of fate it was he, more than any single individual, who was destined to repair the omissions on the economic side of those very military leaders whose policy he had done so much to oppose.

For, strange as it may seem to us, Germany was not really ready for war. She had, it is true, built up enormous armaments, she could and did mobilise an army of unprecedented magnitude, and her navy was in some respects the best equipped in the world, but the whole of her economic system was absolutely unprepared for a prolonged struggle. Her military leaders, relying perhaps on a sudden and easy victory, had wholly neglected to make any adequate preparations for the supplies of essential raw materials, or for the entire transformation of the whole financial and economic activity of the nation which the war very soon demanded. Hence the British blockade which immediately became effective almost threw the whole war machine into a confusion from which it was only saved by the organising genius of Rathenau.

To attempt to tell the story of the department of raw materials which he created, and of the official obstructions and the economic difficulties which he encountered, would be out of place in so short an essay. But a few words will suffice to show the magnitude of the task, which was to collect supplies of all materials (with the exception of food-stuffs and liquid fuels) which were not obtainable permanently or in sufficient quantities within Germany itself. This involved a widespread interference with the private economy of the country which forced the Government (1) to commandeer existing supplies and to see that they were not used for luxury or " civilian " purposes ; (2) to lay hold on all available materials in foreign countries, e.g. neutrals like Sweden, Holland, or Denmark, or in occupied territory like Belgium ; (3) to see that all required commodities were manufactured in sufficient quantities and to develop new processes of manufacture where the old ones were inadequate ; (4) to replace materials which either were scarce or non-existent, by their functional equivalents in the shape of practicable substitutes. This gigantic task, which started with only a dozen materials, grew rapidly until it embraced over a hundred important commodities. A conspicuous example which illustrates the enormous difficulties involved is furnished by nitrates, hitherto imported, the existing supply of which had to be deflected from the farmers against very determined opposition until the process of manufacturing synthetic nitrogen compounds from the air had been developed. Indeed, Rathenau's organisation of nitrate manufacture was one of the decisive events in the war, without which Germany could only have lasted out a comparatively short time.

In order to carry out his task Rathenau invented a peculiar organisation in the shape of the War Industrial Companies, which were a brilliant mixture of State control and commercial enterprise. Their function was to take over the stores of raw materials, look after them, fix their price, and allot them to the different industries as and when they were required. They were self-governing joint-stock corporations whose surplus profits accrued to the State and subject to a certain degree of Government control—a development of the mixed undertaking which had already grown up in certain monopolised industries before the war. Through the formation of these companies large branches of German industry were transformed into self-governing associations constituted by a partnership between the private *entrepreneur* and the State, and it was on the experience gained in the working of these war companies that Rathenau founded some of his most important economic doctrines. Rathenau himself, who had succeeded his father as head of the A.E.G. two years before the war, only remained at the head of the Raw Materials Department for a comparatively short time. He left it in the summer of 1915, eight months after its inception, but not before he had given to it its decisive character and laid down the lines of its future development. *The Times*, a journal little given to hyperbole, described it as " the greatest industrial organisation in the history of the world," and gave full and generous recognition to its creator :

> It is an extraordinary story, this miracle of industry. It is a story which explains the fall of Warsaw and the great Eastern offensive and the impregnable Western line. And when the Falkenhayns, the Mackensens, the Hindenburgs are thought of as great German soldiers, one person must be set beside them, the German business man, Dr. Walther Rathenau.[1]

Rathenau's own personal attitude to the war has often been misrepresented, especially by his enemies and opponents. Count Harry Kessler has described how for the first few days he seemed utterly broken by the catastrophe, but by August 8 he had already begun to formulate his plans for the organisation of German industry to meet the emergency. Nevertheless, he was from the beginning profoundly pessimistic. He feared, rightly enough as the event proved, that the German nation had lost its moral fibre, that its leaders were puffed up with arrogance and its people filled with vanity. While the whole nation was dreaming of impossible conquests and fabulous material gains, he

[1] *The Times*, October 11, 1915.

thought only of peace and the establishment of a
European customs union which was to embrace all
the belligerents. Not that he was a defeatist in the
usual sense of the term, or in the slightest degree disloyal. He worked as hard as any man to gain a victory
for his own nation. But a perusal of his political correspondence shows that, as the months went by, he
became ever more conscious of the incompetence of
Germany's rulers, and though for a while he seems to
have fallen under the spell of Ludendorff's personality,
the intensification of the submarine campaign on which
the Chief of the General Staff and wartime Dictator
laid such stress completely disillusioned him. For he
understood clearly enough that it was bound to bring
the United States into the war on the side of the
Allies, and that unless it achieved a hundred per cent.
success, it was worse than useless. But his protests
were disregarded. President Wilson declared war,
and with the gigantic economic strength of the United
States added in the balance against her, the fate of
Germany was a foregone conclusion. From the beginning of 1917 Rathenau's prognostications on the
course of the war, which were only too quickly verified,
grew ever gloomier, and his only preoccupation was
to seek some termination to the struggle which would
not mean the utter annihilation of his country. During
those bitter war years which followed his retirement
from official life, Rathenau used such leisure as his
vast business interests permitted him in contemplating
the future rather than the present, and completed the
third of his larger works, *Von Kommenden Dingen*—
translated into English under the title *In Days to Come* [1]
—in which he looks forward with a prophetic but
somewhat Utopian eye to the society of the future.

[1] Translation by Eden and Cedar Paul : Messrs. George Allen &
Unwin.

Yet when the final collapse came in 1918, and the German General Staff in a panic demanded an unconditional armistice and the Kaiser tamely abdicated, it was Rathenau, the Jew, not Ludendorff, who was ready to make a last desperate stand. He realised only too clearly that the armistice granted under such conditions would expose a helpless Germany to the vengeance of her enemies, and on October 7 he contributed a stirring article to the *Vossische Zeitung* recommending a *levée en masse* to restore the worn-out fighting front. But it was too late : the German military machine had crumbled to pieces, not, as Ludendorff attempts to maintain, because it had been stabbed in the back by treachery and defeatism at home, but because of its own intrinsic exhaustion. And so the revolution which was to create the short-lived Germany of the Weimar constitution was ushered into the world.

In order to understand Rathenau's attitude to the revolution, it is necessary to consider briefly some of the salient characteristics of his social and economic doctrine, which he published to the world in three considerable volumes and numerous articles and pamphlets. It is of course impossible to give any systematic account of them in this short essay, but some of his principal ideas may perhaps be summarised without too much distortion in the following paragraphs.

While he was still quite a young man working in the dreary little industrial town of Bitterfeld, his imagination had been impressed by the spiritual poverty of the lives of his workmen, condemned to a ceaseless round of monotonous and soul-destroying labour. This condition he conceived to be the inevitable result of mechanisation, the evils of which became almost an obsession with him. For he regarded mechanisation as responsible for the two chief diseases of society—the degradation of the craftsman and his condemnation to a life of virtual servitude and the growth of a soulless and parasitic plutocracy. Now, as we have already observed, Rathenau had undergone a process not unlike that of religious conversion ; like the followers of Dr. Buchman, he had been " changed " ; he had been much influenced by a semi-mystical philosophy which had revealed to him the nature of what he called the soul. By this he did not mean the individual self as such, but rather something more abstract, like the conception of the Kingdom of Heaven. For though all men were according to him capable of *acquiring* a soul, only some were *born* with it. He conceived the soul to be something essentially different from the intellect and immeasurably above it. For the intellect is essentially teleological : it is always directed towards the achievement of some definite purpose, whereas the soul, with its threefold faculties, love, reverence, and awe, has no purposes beyond itself. Most men being occupied with the things of this world never attain a soul, however ethical their conduct, yet all men of good will are capable of acquiring it. The principal object of society is therefore to realise the soul, and the chief impediments to that realisation are mechanisation and the materialistic outlook of which it is at once the product and the source.

The mechanisation of industry, by doing away with the independent craftsman, has robbed the worker of his freedom through the creation of a *rentier* class, to which he is inexorably kept in subjection. For the capitalist, in virtue of his independent means, has command of the labour of others, and the proletarian can only keep himself alive by hiring out his labour, which is largely used to produce luxuries for the rich. It is the hereditary character of modern capitalism which is responsible for this evil. Nevertheless, it is not possible to go back upon the mechanistic evolution of industry ; the only cure is to develop mechanisation still further, and to improve the technical processes of production to such an extent that everyone shall be able to enjoy a decent standard of living and yet have ample leisure to develop his spiritual faculties. This can only be accomplished by a much more thorough process of rationalisation than any that has yet been attempted, which will entail the complete transformation of the present capitalistic system. For capitalism with its insistence upon competition and individualistic effort is doubly wasteful. As might be expected from a system of production which has grown up without any conscious planning, it is almost incredibly inefficient, for even in modern times, the vast majority of goods are still produced in small units greatly inferior technically to the largest and most efficient plants. The individualistic methods of production entail an enormous amount of duplication of capital and redundant processes such as transport between different stages of manufacture—in short, a gigantic waste of economic effort, which could all be eliminated, and has already been eliminated in certain industries, by scientific planning. Moreover, the present distribution of wealth is in itself a cause of waste in so far as the accumulation of effective demand in the hands of the idle rich (chiefly women) leads to a vast expenditure of time and labour on the production of useless and positively harmful luxuries which should be employed in raising the general standard of living by cheapening and improving the commodities consumed by the workers, in shortening their hours of labour, and so in liberating them from economic servitude.

These defects in the capitalist system Rathenau conceived, not like the Marxists as inherent and irremediable, but as curable by a radical social policy, such as a steeply graduated income-tax, high death duties and taxes on luxury-expenditure, combined at the same time with a rapid extension of the monopolistic tendency inherent in a large-scale production. The logical conclusion of these developments he envisaged in *Things to Come* as the complete rationalisation and concentration of industry into a number of autonomous units which could perhaps be best described as a cross between the modern and the mediæval Guild. These units or corporations will be of two different kinds— horizontal and vertical. The horizontal associations will embrace all undertakings of a similar nature, e.g. cotton-spinning, weaving, steel-rolling, locomotive building, etc. They will be responsible for buying raw materials and marketing the products of the single undertakings which participate in them, and for the distribution of orders and the control of production generally. The function of the vertical associations will be to co-ordinate the activities of horizontal associations which go to compose a single industry. They will not be directly concerned in production or marketing but in planning, forecasting supply and demand, fixing standards and specifications, regulating prices, and so forth. These associations will not be Government departments, but independent monopolistic trusts endowed with statutory powers by the State and subject to a certain degree of Government supervision. They will be definitely privately owned, but their profits will be limited ; after paying a fixed rate of interest on capital, the surplus will be divided between the producers and the State, and part of it will be used to raise wages or to lower prices. They will be managed by Boards composed of representatives of *entrepreneurs*, labour, and the Government.

By this type of organisation, which was largely

modelled on the war trading companies and industrial
control boards, Rathenau conceived that the produc-
tivity of industry would be enormously increased ; but
the social problem, the problem of the general direction
of economic energies, would still remain unsolved.
The ideal he was seeking was something much wider
than capitalism *in excelsis* subjected to a certain amount
of social control : what he was aiming at was the
deproletarianising of the working classes and the building up of a classless State. This, he insisted, could
not be brought about by Marxist methods, which he
criticised very severely both for their impracticability
and for their spiritual inadequacy. Hence he repudiated any form of communism or any attempt to
create a complete equality in the distribution of wealth,
which he regarded as unnatural. At the same time he
was convinced of the necessity for a much more even
distribution of wealth than that at present existing.
Hence his emphasis on the need of strict measures of
social control over the expenditure of the individual
and his insistence on taxation as an instrument for this
purpose. For without neglecting the differences in
ability and character with which men are born into
the world, he sought to destroy the inequality of
opportunity which the transmission of hereditary
wealth perpetuates. In the last resort it was not on
material but on spiritual values that his heart was set,
and his whole social schemes were aimed, not so much
at prosperity as at salvation, the realisation of the life
of the soul. The guild organisation was to be, not
merely a producer's trust, but a vehicle of the corporate life, the final object of which was to be the
spiritualisation of labour. This ideal presented itself
as an all but insoluble problem, for he was unable to
escape from the conception, so prominent in the thought
of Plato and Aristotle, that material labour is as such

degrading, and the only solution which he could find lay in the further development of mechanisation and the equalisation of labour, i.e. the sharing of manual and brain work. He therefore put forward, in a book published soon after the outbreak of the revolution, the proposal that every German should compulsorily undergo a year's training in manual work. But in the end he was forced to the conclusion that the spiritualisation of labour would only be attained as the result of a long process of development :

> It will only be completed when it has become superfluous ; when, that is to say, the true meaning of labour has returned, and this will happen when mechanisation has conquered itself.

This curious mixture of romantic Utopianism with a profound insight into the formative tendencies of modern social development was greeted by his contemporaries with a good deal of hostile criticism. Rathenau was not slow to experience the proverbial fate of prophets, and being particularly thin-skinned, especially where his writings were concerned, he suffered acutely. His enemies attempted to expose him as a traitor to his class and a humbug, a multi-millionaire business-man posing as a *Christ en frac*, a " parlour-bolshevik " preaching apostolic poverty from a palace. There was indeed just sufficient truth in this accusation to make it particularly telling. For Rathenau, though not unduly ostentatious, was certainly no ascetic : he gave free rein to his artistic tastes, never stinted himself in the acquisition of beautiful things, and thoroughly enjoyed travelling *en suite* from capital to capital as the financial Nabob. In fact, like many other great and good men, he had his foibles. Moreover, as the war dragged on, the ferocity as well as the anti-Semitism of the German people grew more and more violent.   Being neither a pacifist nor a jingo Rathenau felt himself more and more isolated—a voice crying in the wilderness.   When the revolution broke out he was thoroughly unpopular : by the Right he was hated as a Jew and a defeatist, by the Left as a capitalist and a war-monger on account of his protest against the Armistice.   In 1919, hoping to retrieve his position, he joined the Liberal German Democratic Party and attempted to found a Democratic People's League, but, greatly to his chagrin, he failed to secure his election to the National Assembly : and an even worse blow was to follow—his name was struck off the Commission for the Socialisation of German In-dustry.   Moreover, when he was nominated by an incautious admirer as the first President of the *Reich*, his name was greeted with an outburst of laughter, a fate which was also accorded to another distinguished candidate, Field-Marshal von Hindenburg.   It is not altogether surprising therefore that he was disgusted with the revolution, which he criticised as wanting in moral leadership and as a sterile replica of the worn-out *bourgeois* democracy and gas-and-water socialism. But in spite of his anger and disappointment at being excluded from the founding of the new Germany, Rathenau did not refuse assistance to the Government when the time arrived for facing the Allied demands on account of reparations.   He was taken by Dr. Wirth, the Finance Minister, as an expert to the Spa Con-ference (July 1920), and among his colleagues was Stinnes, the uncrowned King of Germany.   Stinnes was a big blustering person whose only idea of policy was blank defiance and damn the consequences. Rathenau, on the other hand, wanted to negotiate, for he considered that once negotiations could be started at all it would only be a matter of time before the Allies began to realise that their demands could not possibly be fulfilled. Hence, the only chance for Germany of obtaining justice was to fulfil the Treaty as far as she could, and to trust to her diplomacy to obtain eventual revision of the most oppressive stipulations imposed at Versailles. After a great battle Stinnes was routed and Rathenau's views prevailed ; and so the policy of fulfilment later carried out by Stresemann was adopted by the German Government, to the fury of the Nationalists and the broken remnant of the officer-class.

It is not necessary here to follow successive steps in the discreditable and tortuous story of reparations with the interminable wranglings and ultimatums which led finally to the occupation of the Ruhr and the collapse of the German currency. The dragon's teeth sowed by Clemenceau and Poincaré have produced an abundant harvest in the last two years and the end is not yet. It is difficult even now, in the height of the feeling aroused by the conduct of the Nazi Government, to realise the almost incredible hatred and suspicion with which the whole German nation was regarded by its conquerors, who refused for years to treat with its representatives on terms at all resembling equality, or to apply to them even the most ordinary courtesies of diplomatic usage. On the German side feeling was scarcely less bitter : the nation had yielded to *force majeure* for fear of worse to come, and there were few if any who felt the slightest moral obligation to fulfil the onerous terms of the Peace Treaty, while the Nationalists, defeated but defiant, were openly resorting to assassination as a method of ridding themselves of the traitors, who had consented to yield to such humiliating terms. The position of Rathenau and of the Wirth Government was therefore extremely delicate. Without admitting the justice of the contract of Versailles, they had to make a reasonable effort at fulfilment in order to avoid, not only the imputation of bad faith, but also the application of further force on the part of the Allies, while at the same time sparing their own people as much hardship by way of taxation, etc., as they could. Hence the easiest solution was to depreciate the currency, and for want of any more courageous device to resort to the policy of inflation which finally wrought such havoc after the invasion of the Ruhr. Upon Rathenau, who entered the Wirth cabinet as Minister for Reconstruction and later succeeded Rosen as Foreign Minister, fell the twin task of convincing the Reparations Commission and the Supreme Council that Germany was attempting to fulfil her obligations, and of persuading an exasperated and demoralised nation, torn with fierce internal dissensions, that he was upholding at once its interest and its honour. There were moments when he seemed almost on the point of success in accomplishing this double miracle. His direct negotiations on deliveries in kind with M. Loucheur, which resulted in the Wiesbaden agreements, seemed to promise at least a partial solution to the reparation tangle. But the French industrialists jibbed at the proposal, which would have meant that to a large extent the devastated areas would be reconstructed by German industry. Moreover, at the critical moment in the middle of the Cannes Conference, the slightly more conciliatory Briand Government fell, to be replaced by the implacable Poincaré just after German feeling had been still more exacerbated by the allocation of the Silesian coalfields to Poland.

Meanwhile, Mr. Lloyd George, who was growing more and more alarmed at the economic chaos in Europe, in creating which he had played such an important and, as he has attempted to persuade us, unwilling part, had persuaded the Allies to summon a conference at Genoa in April 1922 to discuss the pacification and reconstruction of Europe. To this conference were summoned no less than 29 States, including not only Germany but also Soviet Russia, which was anxious to gain readmission into the concert of Europe in order to raise a loan, while at the same time profiting by her partial rehabilitation to further the cause of world revolution. But the failure of the conference had already been assured beforehand by M. Poincaré, who insisted on excluding from the agenda all reference to the question of Reparations, and used every means in his power to prevent Germany being treated on a level of equality with the Great Powers. After a tussle he managed to exclude the Germans from certain private conversations between the Allied Powers and the Russians. His aim was to persuade the Russians to demand reparations from Germany, which they were entitled to do under the Treaty of Versailles, and to use the proceeds to pay interest on their pre-war French loans. Rathenau, who had some months previously been negotiating a treaty with Russia, which he had purposely refrained from signing in order not to prejudice the chances of the Conference to effect a general settlement, was naturally perturbed. Hearing of the Poincaré plan he attempted to explain his difficulties to Lloyd George, who refused to see him until too late, thus wounding his vanity, always a tender organ, and arousing his suspicions still further. He was consequently an easy prey to the blandishments of Tchitcherin, who succeeded in stampeding him into signing a separate Treaty with the Soviets at Rapallo, which finally wrecked the Conference.[1]

---

[1] Lord D'Abernon in his Diary sums up the proceedings in a masterly epitome :

" The story of the Genoa Conference and of the Treaty of Rapallo has often been told. But it has never been told rightly. The inner workings, which inspired events, have remained unknown. In last analysis, it was a

The Treaty of Rapallo appears to have been in itself quite an inoffensive arrangement. There is no evidence that it contained any secret military agreements : it merely provided for a resumption of diplomatic intercourse and an abandonment of all claims arising out of the war. It was, in fact, essentially a Peace Treaty. But it was a blunder of the first order—because it confirmed France in her intransigeance and sacrificed all the chances of an Anglo-German *rapprochement* for a diplomatic support which, in his heart of hearts, Rathenau knew to be worthless, and to the world at large it appeared merely as a sinister alliance between the two pariahs of Europe. Nevertheless, even if he was no Talleyrand, he had succeeded in placing Germany once more upon the diplomatic map of Europe, and extorting even from those foreign statesmen who trusted him least an unwilling admiration for his brilliant abilities. But Rapallo was not popular even in Germany itself. As Lord D'Abernon's diary

conflict of three vanities—Lloyd George, Rathenau, and Poincaré. The last named was determined the Conference should not succeed—that Lloyd George should not attain his purpose of conciliating Germany, of bringing Russia into the European conclave. Lloyd George . . . might have found in Rathenau an ardent convert to this policy, and the two in combination might have carried the day—and alter history for better or worse. But Vanity came in. Lloyd George had met Poincaré a few weeks before at Boulogne. Lloyd George had been conciliatory. Poincaré had been truculent. Commenting on this matter in the Reichstag, Rathenau said that Lloyd George had been defeated by Poincaré. This was not true ; had it been ten times true, it would have been a grave blunder on the eve of Genoa to say it. Lloyd George read this speech ; he naturally resented it— resented it all the more that he had been in friendly touch with Rathenau. When the two arrived at Genoa, Lloyd George avoided giving Rathenau an interview, even if he did not refuse to receive him.

" Rathenau's vanity was wounded, his suspicions were aroused. If he was not received by Lloyd George, it must be that deep plots were being hatched between Allies and Russians. Germany would be isolated. Rathenau would appear ridiculous, and return to Berlin as a German delegate who had been neglected, outwitted, and befooled. The Russians, with their accustomed skill, played on these feelings. Rathenau and the rest of the German delegation were stampeded ; the Rapallo Treaty was signed. *Vanitas vanitatum et omnia vanitas.*"—D'ABERNON, *An Ambassador of Peace*, vol. i, pp. 39-40.

shows, it was intensely distasteful to President Ebert, and it only served to inflame the hostility of the Right, already intensely nervous of the Communists within, against Rathenau himself.   Indeed, it was to prove the final signing of his death-warrant.

Ever since he had taken office in the summer of 1921 against the solemn entreaty of his mother, Rathenau had realised that he was a doomed man.   Yet with Oriental fatalism he refused police precautions.   He knew full well the strength and the bitterness of his enemies, but he was too proud and too sensitive to forestall them.   Although forewarned he refused to be forearmed, and he seemed almost deliberately to court the martyr's crown.   After Genoa he had not long to wait.   As far back as the end of 1920 Ludendorff, anxious to conceal his own responsibility for the collapse of 1918, had raised the hue and cry by deliberately misinterpreting some incautious phrases in Rathenau's essay on the Kaiser, and month by month Stinnes and Helfferich had fanned the flames.   In June the end came with dramatic suddenness.   On the night of the 27th he had met his adversary Stinnes in Berlin at the house of the American Ambassador, Houghton.   He had talked with him far into the night, and seemed at last to have reached a basis for future understanding. The next morning on his way to the Foreign Office he was assassinated while driving in his open car by a band of Nationalist youths led by an ex-naval officer named Kern, of that Nordic type which he so admired.   This horrible act of stupid and insensate vengeance deprived German public life of its outstanding figure, one who had proved, almost for the first time, that it was possible to be both a great German and a Jew.   Once more the spirit of assassination showed its tragic blindness, which so often strikes at friends in mistake for foes.

MAX REINHARDT

BY ALAN PRYCE-JONES

MAX REINHARDT

MAX REINHARDT

By Alan Pryce-Jones

I

I THINK it was my friend Mr. Cattaui who was talking
one evening of the curious manner in which particular
peoples have evoked a particular response from the
Jewish race. If we put the matter negatively we can
see at once how in England, for instance, there has
never been a great Jewish composer. Or, since the
subject of great English composers is a touchy one, we
may notice that, until lately, there has been no great
Jewish painter in France (nor was the chief exception,
Modigliani, a Frenchman by birth). It would seem
that, with their immense adaptability, the Jews have
usually taken out of a country that predilection which
gives the greatest bias to its people and have proceeded to inform it with a Jewish ardour, as constant
and forcible a shaping influence as the Roman Catholic
ardour, or, in a minor degree, the Calvinist ardour of
New England.

Thus it is not surprising that the activities of the
Jews in England have usually been absorbed by commerce, since the ideal of wealth is held up more per-
sistently to every Aryan child in England than on the
Continent, where wealth is admired, not as an ideal in
itself, but as a means to obtaining an ideal. To
France the typical Jewish contribution is intellectual
analysis—I (and M. Cattaui) are thinking of Proust
and Bergson ; to Germany creative music—I am told
that Heine can almost be included here as the most
musical of poets ; to the United States a system of
racketeering so well organised that at one time it
seemed likely to revive a dying oligarchic tradition ;

and to Austria the creative theatre ; which can conveniently be personified in Max Goldmann, whom we know better as Max Reinhardt.

Before we consider Reinhardt in detail it may be worth while to inquire what is the specially Jewish flavour, the international Jewish bias if you like, which is applied to these various national interests ? For there can be no question that Jewish influence strongly affects whatever it touches, whether we think of its manifestations—according to our prejudice—as the eddies set up by a stone thrown into still water or as the coils of a boa constrictor. Is it important that Proust and Lord Melchett, So-and-So the gangster, and Reinhardt are Jews ?

The Jewish contribution of each to his activities is seriousness ; each of them has converted his business into an art, if it was not an art already. And when we say that the Jews are eminently artistic we mean that they have the special faculties of absorption and unity of purpose which among Aryans are generally reserved for the arts—where they are called praiseworthy—and not for the business of living—where they are condemned as over-professional, or grasping. Probably it is their unwillingness to discriminate between professional and amateur activities—in a phrase, their skill in living—which has brought Jews, not only into a position at the head of art and finance, but also into periodical bad odour. The world complains of the dumping of Jewish capability from the same reliance on a different code as Great Britain, in 1933, complains of Japanese dumped manufactures.

The fact that he is a Jew has, therefore, directed the work of Reinhardt and through him, the whole trend of the theatre, to some extent. His serious brilliance, his thoroughness in supervising every detail to get the right total effect, are, in part at least, the legacy of his race.

II

The German theatre, at any rate since the time of
Goethe, has been kept at a higher pitch of theatrical art
than elsewhere in Europe. What is more, in Bavaria
and the Tyrol, and in that part of Austria where
Catholic and peasant concepts were preserved least
spotted by outside influences, an ancient dramatic
tradition—now, I believe, not best shown at Ober-
ammergau—was unbroken throughout the nineteenth
century, and free of a certain German heaviness into
the bargain. The Austrians themselves are proverbi-
ally a volatile race, easily moved, and therefore fond of
the theatre ; and many is the old gentleman whose
eye, hooded with the cigar smoke which curls round
a leather-buttoned club chair, beams anew at the re-
collection of pre-war Vienna, of the music, the dancing,
the spectacular and theatrical gaieties which were the
nursery of Reinhardt's imagination.

Herr Reinhardt is now sixty years old, and so far
from moribund that I do not mean to disclose—ignor-
ance can creditably be covered by scruples—personal
details of him ; and the main facts are so bare that
they had better be put together at once. He was born
at Baden, near Vienna, on September 9, 1873. In
youth he was apprenticed to a banking business, but,
at the age of seventeen, became an actor on the Vienna
stage, taking for his first part that of Spiegelberg in the
Robbers of Schiller. He played in a theatre at which,
to appear at all, the actors had to pay the manager.
Later he went to Salzburg, and there happened to be
noticed by the Berlin producer, Otto Brahm, then the
most influential name in the German theatre, who was
touring the provinces in search of talent. Reinhardt
specialised in elderly character parts, and so impressed
Brahm that he was engaged for the following season

in Berlin. Later he tried to cancel the contract, but Brahm was insistent, and so he found himself, in Berlin of 1894, a promising young actor.

Before long, with a few friends, he began to organise a sort of private cabaret, a skittish unpretentious affair, largely consisting of parody. Eventually the public was admitted, a cabaret, *Schall und Rauch*, was formed, and proved so successful that in 1902 Reinhardt was able to open the Kleines Theater and break away from Brahm altogether. Nineteen hundred and five was the next important year in his life, for then first he scored a real success with the *Midsummer Night's Dream*. Since then his career is merely a list of productions. In Berlin he directed, not only the Kleines Theater, but also the Deutsches Theater and the vast Schauspielhaus, in which the *Miracle* and other such gigantic productions were done ; and he also found time for several successful American tours. Latterly, however, Reinhardt has severed all connection with Germany, whether because of cabals or excessive taxation, and, after a period in Vienna, has mainly devoted himself to founding and supervising the annual festival at Salzburg, first mooted during the war.

It did not look, in the late 'nineties, as if this young Austrian Jew would accomplish so much, or indeed anything. After the salutary influence of Goethe was spent the German theatre, though so closely linked to the Court life of each separate State that it never needed other patronage, became dulled by its own prosperity. It was not until Georg, Duke of Saxe-Meiningen, took his famous company of players on tour that it made any conscious effort to free itself from " the way things had always been done."

It then became the fashion most to value realism at any cost. The stage must be a room with the fourth wall removed ; and since drabness is the principal

ingredient of actual life, it followed that drabness became the most popular quality in the theatre ; the
theatre must, as a first aim, avoid the " theatrical."
Of this manner of production Otto Brahm was the
chief exponent.

His reaction from the subfusc of an excessive
naturalism led Reinhardt to cabaret, the brightest of
theatrical departments, and eventually to the Little
Theatre movement, which has done more than any
other for the intelligent playgoer.   It is only, however,
with the greatest reluctance that Reinhardt has even
admitted the existence of such a person—not out of
despite towards the intelligent, but out of a surprising
respect for the *average* spectator. A pre-eminent object
of his work has been to create an audience, an entity,
and in that there must be a minimum of individual
reactions, whereas the Brahm method of production
encouraged each member of the audience to react personally to the naturalistic scene on the stage (and
indeed quite how any impression worth receiving can be
received by a corporate audience I do not understand).

The success of the Kleines Theater encouraged
Reinhardt to widen his scope.   The *Midsummer
Night's Dream* of 1905 was a production which, however we may flinch now from its fancifulness, revealed
to Berlin at that time a new range of colour and movement, as startling as a Liszt rhapsody in the middle of
a sedately somnolent concert.   For the task of the
theatre, says Reinhardt, is " to lift the word out of
the sepulchre of the book," and henceforward it was
exclusively with that aim that he worked.

Nobody was ever less of a " highbrow "—one is
sometimes driven to use that odious word—or less
dogmatic.   He knew that the first object of a theatre
is to entertain—perhaps so long a preoccupation with
vaudeville has left its mark—and only the second

(please Heaven, invisible) object, to instruct ; thereby reversing the emphasis given by Goethe, the earlier genius of the German stage. And possibly not the least excellent result of Reinhardt's work has been to liberate stage-production from the dogmatic, to encourage flexibility by showing again and again that " every masterpiece has its own style." This may seem obvious enough to stick out a yard ; nevertheless, it has needed the efforts of men still alive—Edward Gordon Craig not least—to jolt the preliminary attitude of a producer away from nineteenth-century routine.

In 1906 Reinhardt did a notable production of *A Winter's Tale*, and another of *Ghosts*. In his production of the latter he took something from expressionism, if only the setting of Edvard Munch, and, for the former, his inspiration from Gordon Craig, who is, in more respects than one, the source of Reinhardt's success. This need not imply plagiarism on his part. The essence of Gordon Craig's method is to strip the theatre of its inessentials and to recreate the stage *in terms of the theatre*. To reach the same just conclusion is simply a sign of perception, not of plagiarism, in whomever-it-may-be. When Gordon Craig has once laid down the necessity of a theatrical theatre (as one might exhort a backward art to think at last in terms of itself) the picture he paints of a theatrical theatre is often too fantastic to be convincing. Read *On the Art of the Theatre*, a book to be read by anyone who likes good books, irrespective of a taste for the theatre, and you will find that a natural dislike of that being spoken which is better read has made him denounce the very presence of words, or even actors, on the stage. Though deliberately fantastic, and not altogether unfunny, this description of a *décor* from *The Theatre Advancing* is only the extremest projection from a point of view which has created all Reinhardt's spectacles :

Cannot you imagine a stage held up by supports as thin as storks' legs, trimmed with the plumage of birds, and here and there a long string of pearls hanging ? Powder, beautiful powder all over the floor, perfumes—but here I am taking on not only the place but the scene, costume, and all.

Little tapers of the finest wax. Not enough tapers ?—then bring in a thousand more in silver sticks. No, I think we will have crystal. Each candle perfumed, and perfuming the air as it burns. Such a quantity of beautiful lace, everything spick and span—and perishable.

The actors are to be—

just something frail—always something fragile. Pale, I fancy them, never speaking above a whisper ; always singing, as it were, with the mute on.

By now we are well out of the realm of the commercial theatre, and therefore out of the realm of Reinhardt ; for, though Gordon Craig has entirely renounced the commercial theatre and is bound in consequence to be a theorist, no more, Reinhardt is a producer who continues to produce. And those who have to judge him simply by his London production of the *Miracle*, who are ready to call that a dreadful affair, tawdrily sentimental and not even pleasant to the eye, those who are ready to dismiss Reinhardt as a revue producer, need only look at the list of his productions.

From Sophocles to Gorky there is hardly a great play which he has not touched. Whether it be an immense production of *Oedipus Rex* which toured Northern Europe for two years, or a minutely sensitive production of Gorky's *Nachtasyl*, he has brought the same impressively vivid imagination to each. Shakespeare, Molière, Strindberg, Goethe, Ibsen, Shaw, Wedekind, Tolstoy, Maeterlinck, Goldoni, Euripides, Offenbach, Aristophanes, are only names which peg out the corners of his province.

III

The realistic school looked no farther than the
nearest sitting-room for its scenic ideal.   For a change
there were the luridly realistic fantasies of Wagner, the
green-lit collapsible anvils, gas-breathing dragons, and
canvas waves on the Rhine.   The moment you saw
the curtain rise on one of the forest scenes you knew
that the real forest of the gods was exactly like that.
Wagner had been there and had remembered everything.   So you could listen and watch, secure in the
knowledge that the stage scene was perfectly
realistic.

If, on the other hand, you went to *A Winter's Tale*
in 1906, you were by no means so comfortable.   For
example, the scenes in Bohemia were painted in an
entirely different style from the others.   You were in a
world of children's toys, almost of *Petrouchka*.   It was
quite certain that Reinhardt had not made the same
physical journey to Bohemia as Wagner to Walhalla ;
he had travelled with his mind into a Bohemian atmosphere and—which was the most exhausting part—you
had to do the same, because otherwise the setting was
not " like " Bohemia, nor " like " the rest of the play.
In fact, you had to use your mind twice over.

This is where Reinhardt's conception of the audience
as an entity seems to fail, since Bohemia must be a
different place for every member, however sharp the
conception which the producer may have of his own
Bohemia (though perhaps the part played by *Masaniello*
in the independence movement in Belgium, or the reception of *Hernani*, may be taken as evidence of the
force which can be expelled from the stage into an
auditorium).   Yet in less subtle productions—for
Reinhardt's elasticity allowed him to range from the
classics to musical comedy—his extraordinary talent

for treating a play as a play and not as a piece of homeless literature was ever sure of presenting a world which would at once be coherent to an audience.

To this end he inquired into the theatre of all periods and countries, and, again like Gordon Craig, discovered the immense resources of the Oriental theatre and of the puppet show. The revolving stage, for instance, though used before Reinhardt's day at the Munich Residenztheater for Mozart performances, was originally a Japanese device of which Reinhardt made the first wide modern use when one was built into the Deutsches Theater, formerly under Brahm's directorship, which he took over in 1905. (Incidentally, when he fostered an intelligent use of this device nearly thirty years ago, he was not to know that eventually it would be used in such productions as one lately r-1t on the Coliseum stage in London, the climax of which was what I took to be the St. Pancras Hotel rapidly revolving. Later it was discovered to have been Venice.)

From the intellectual No drama of Japan to the modern work of Stanislawsky in Moscow, from Court masques to musical comedy, Reinhardt collected those notes, so to speak, to which he could refer for any problem. And with this wide perspective before him he was saved from any danger of reliance on a formula. He was able—I find myself writing of him, for no special reason, in the past tense—to approach a masterpiece or a mere " show " as though it were not only a first performance, but also a wholly original demand on his technique.

This technique, according to Mr. Kahane, is evolved in three stages. First, Reinhardt takes the manuscript with him on a solitary holiday and allows himself to make a mental picture of the focal points of his production. Then he draws an exact outline of the available space at his disposal ; then fills in every detail of movement and colour.

There is an argument in Boswell which ends thus :

Johnson : . . . Do you respect a rope-dancer or a ballad-singer ?

Boswell : No, sir, but we respect a great player, as a man who can conceive lofty sentiments and can express them gracefully.

Johnson : What, sir, a fellow who claps a hump on his back and a lump on his leg, and cries, " *I am Richard the Third* " ? Nay, sir, a ballad-singer is a higher man, for he does two things ; he repeats and he sings : there is both recitation and music in his performance ; the player only recites.

The voice of Dr. Johnson and the voice of Gordon Craig are oddly alike ; but Reinhardt differs from either. Having worked out the inanimate part of his production, for him there is no " fellow." His actors are not dictated to ; at a rehearsal, if thorough, he is ever quiet. It follows, from this, that the actor has in the end to create his own part, helped only by the cohesive atmosphere which Reinhardt is able to weave round every facet of a production and by a personal force which, simply from his presence at a rehearsal, seems able to fire the players—though he may scarcely make a suggestion—with a new ability. A catalogue is an unexciting testimonial to success, but an extract of the actors whose success is due to Reinhardt, or mainly to Reinhardt, is impressive. Jannings, Werner Krauss, Lillibil Ibsen, and Elizabeth Bergner are a fair quartet to begin with. Moissi, the most famous of German Hamlets, and Max Pallenberg, who began as a musical-comedy actor, became known in his theatres ; and Lubitsch started his own career as a " super " in the *Miracle*.

Such introductions as we are allowed in England of more experimental schools of drama and more stylised methods of acting may leave a suspicion that Reinhardt, as well as other pre-war reconstructors of the theatre, are falling out of date. It may be argued that those artists whom he has definitely inspired—von Hofmannsthal, Richard Strauss, and Hauptmann—are not artists of the first water ; and that the ability to make a satisfactory spectacle in a space varying from Olympia to a theatre seating a few hundred, needs little more than imagination controlled by a sense of proportion.

But then there is no room for what is commonly called artists of the first water in the theatre, since the theatre demands, for a theatrical masterpiece, a good leavening of the second-rate. Theatrical first-rate, to be given its due as such, is second-rate anywhere else. That is to say, *The Death of Procris*—or even Manet's immense *Execution of the Emperor Maximilian* is a second-rate theatrical conception in comparison with the pastoral, or impassioned, settings of the late Mr. Harker ; and the entirety of *Der Rosenkavalier*, just *because* it is music less good than *Tristan und Isolde* fitted to words less good than *Romeo and Juliet*, is a better dramatic entertainment than either. Nor is there any indication that the various " trends " of the modern stage can ever lead to anything more refreshing than intellectualised boredom, unless the theatre keeps its eyes firmly on the slightly, the ever so slightly, second-rate—as the second-rate is viewed from an armchair.

I have said that Reinhardt is no theorist, and I do not suppose that he has hampered himself with many ideals beyond that of providing good entertainments. It would be easy to say that one of his talents is to be able " to free himself from his own ideas," or to congratulate him on his catholicity. I prefer to think that

he is entirely spontaneous in applying his knowledge
and experience to that cheapening and underlining of
the passions which we call great drama, or to the purely
delightful assaults on the nerves which are supposed
to need a good dinner in the van.

Let us look for a moment at the most famous of
Reinhardt's productions, the *Miracle*. Effective ? Yes,
we must call it effective. A London theatre is transformed into a cathedral of the most horrible pseudo-
Gothic, but most people will like that, and anyhow it
is not directly Reinhardt's fault (*If only you'd seen it
at Olympia*, everyone is saying). Although the play is
to be entirely a-moral, if not frankly immoral, we have
got to think it very beautiful, and so the religious music,
the nuns processing with their candles, and the incense
trickling over the footlights are excellent devices for
stirring a *theatrically* aweful emotion—for you are not
going to tell me that there is any emotion there comparable to what we can feel from book or picture composed under the unique impulse of one mind ?

Above all, we are to feel that what we are watching
is very beautiful ; so the colours must be vivid and the
grouping have a certain statuesque quality which will
help us to keep in mind that what we see is allegorical.
The music must not be very good, or we shall have to
attend to it, but it must sound rather beautiful. Since
there are to be no words there must be a great deal of
vigorous action, but action grotesque or convention-
alised or merely rhythmic, lest we approach the story
too closely to real life, and discover it to be, like so
many of the best plays in the world, real nonsense in
those terms. Lastly, we must be encouraged not to
think (I begin to see what Reinhardt means when he
demands a corporate audience) but to feel as hotly as
may be ; to feel how beautiful it all is, not more
concisely than that.

It is hard to see how the trick could have been better done. Fault-finders, of whom I am often ashamed to own myself one, hate approving a popular artistic success, especially when the measure of its success is purely its æsthetic effect on a crowd. To the fault-finders, then, the *Miracle* gave no pleasure whatever ; yet even they could not but admire the accuracy of each appeal to an emotional sense of beauty, the ease with which the sordid, the meretricious, or the plain silly, was made to seem, for a moment, beautiful. " If only you'd seen it at Olympia," the audience told one another, and I cannot doubt that in such a vast amphitheatre the appeals would have been more compulsive, because the theatrical would have been so astonishingly magnified, the second-rate have gained a new value with its new stature—the stature envisaged, when he first planned the production, by Reinhardt.

But what puts Reinhardt in a class by himself as a producer is that he is no less at ease in staging an intellectual play in a small space for a small audience. A number of producers can make an excellent job of *The Father*, but they cannot go straight on to make as good a job of something which every newspaper will describe as " mammoth." Art, Reinhardt has said, is conscious impression on the public ; and he has realised that the best way of making that impression is : first, to hold the reins in his own pair of hands rather than to distribute them among stage-directors, chief actors, machinists, and those who arrange settings and lights ; second, to fuse the actors, while allowing them as much latitude as will cram into his picture, into a unity. To a certain point this must be the aim of every director ; where Reinhardt differs is to allow, once he has made his picture, so much scope for the talents of those whom he is directing.

IV

During the war, as I have said, a plan was made to build a great festival theatre in Salzburg. It was an enthusiastic plan, and pursued with greater enthusiasm after the war. There was to be an atmosphere almost of holiness in the precincts; a phrase about " the Temple of the Drama " was freely used; workshops, subsidiary halls, and dramatic schools were to be built; and nobody had any money at all.

The choice of Salzburg was not altogether a sentimental one, though Reinhardt, who was close-linked to the plan from its beginning, was an Austrian and had begun his own career there. For it is almost at the centre of the railway-systems of Europe and has, besides, a strangely dramatic atmosphere in which every view is a " set."

Among the mountains a sharp wooded hill stands, with a shallow stony river at its foot, and upon it a castle, galleried, huge, theatrically stern. By the river, spread over a curve, are streets and squares which might at any hour be transformed into tents or hung with the flags of visiting notables. Straight lines are masked by stucco plumes, windows are moulded into billowy slits which recall the prow of a ceremonial barge. The set-pieces of the town—an Italian cathedral, wide spaces backed by a colonnade or turning about a fountain in which vast bronze horses struggle against the feeblest of water jets—are backed by the right labyrinth of worn steps up a cliff, tunnels cut through the rock and turned almost into grottos by the heavy rococo of their entrances; and miniature scenes, as stiff and childishly classical as the wood-engravings of Rome which turn up in second-hand portfolios.

The Temple of the Drama does not yet exist; but the whole town has been laid under contribution. The outdoor riding-school of the Archbishops' Palace has been made into an outdoor theatre ; and a tolerable theatre has been made of its indoor neighbour—though the low pitch of the roof spoils the acoustics and the wooden chairs like to make themselves heard as the audience begins to loll. In the latter opera is staged, and in the former such elaborate productions as the second part of *Faust*, in which a village or a garden, thanks to the great size of the arena, can be given almost its true proportions.

The square in front of the cathedral is used for von Hofmannsthal's *Jedermann* (what a superb stroke of Reinhardt's, to have the bells of the town churches peal and voices cry from the towers ! Now do you see how necessary the second-rate is to first-rate " theatre " ?) ; a tiny open-air eighteenth-century theatre is used for such operas as *Bastien et Bastienne* ; and other churches are used for plays with a suitably religious background.

Although Reinhardt does not himself produce all of this multiple festival, he is always at hand ; and, from the large house at Leopoldskron where he lives, presides where he does not directly command. The festival, unless political reasons destroy it, is now established ; but its success is almost entirely due to the prestige, the first years of real work, and the present super-vision, of Reinhardt ; the bait of whose evening fêtes —Leopoldskron is better suited to magnificence by night than ordinary comfort by day—attracts those of the rich who, if they are not too exhausted by the night before, beat time during the first act of an opera and sleep during the rest.

(Reinhardt has brought a growing sum of money to Salzburg ; his festival has given a fresh reputation to Austrian art as surely as Proust has given a fresh reputation to the French novel. Yet, should a

Fascist Government gain control, because he is a Jew that will be forgotten ; and, since a Fascist Government is not impossible,[1] Leopoldskron is to be let, and an outlet in another country would not, we gather, be refused. The point need not be elaborated further.)

While he was planning this festival, Reinhardt, in search of a new field, converted the Redoutensaal of the late Imperial Palace at Vienna into a theatre for a revival of the Commedia dell'Arte—a theatre hung with superb tapestries and designed for a small, and intelligent, audience. By touching this world, the world to which Mr. Coward's comedies aspire, Reinhardt completed the circle of his activities ; he could now say that there was no branch of the theatre which he had not attempted successfully.

I found myself above writing in the past tense ; and here again. So the pen slips, unconsciously aware that Reinhardt has made his contribution. Each new production can stand on its own legs as an entertainment, but it will not reveal to us anything new. Indeed, in the end the influence of Reinhardt will probably consist of a general recognition of the stupidity of all formulas ; it will not be because of his innovations, his " sense of ensemble," his introduction of, say, the revolving stage, that he will be remembered, but because he showed that it was possible to approach any kind of a play with a free mind, to find a special technique for each.

Can that, too, be a Jewish quality: to look at things as they are ? to watch the universe (if Einstein) with new eyes, to watch the correlation of heart and brain (if Proust) with new eyes, or with new eyes the bare space of the stage ? That is not a

[1] November, 1933.

rhetorical question, for an exhilarating realism is the least common factor of Jews of genius.

In the last few years the chief business of Europe has become propaganda, the chief export, and the chief recreation. This has naturally enough been reflected in the theatre. In Russia we know the propagandist tendency to shift the emphasis, even of Shakespeare, so as to drive the interest into political channels ; until even *Romeo and Juliet*, I have read, become the protagonists of a struggle between pro-letarait and bourgeoisie.

In England, except for a certain amount of propa-ganda for various vices or for the blind muddle in which " ordinary people " are happy to live, the propagandist theatre exists almost entirely in the works of Shaw, who, with Shakespeare and Wedekind, forms a trilogy of Reinhardt's most frequently performed and most popular playwrights. Propaganda plays the Baptist to Interference, and it may be that the theatre will shortly become a political power not only in Russia. If so, it will be one of the many spheres in which the Jewish world can play a valuable international part since, though it is now commonly accepted that interference *quatenus* interference is a principal glory of civilised man, it is as well to offset that which arises from national propaganda by an insistence on the least domestic, the least petty, aspects of mankind.

From that angle, Reinhardt can be called to the side of the angels. Among all his productions he has not, so far as I can read or remember, produced rubbish, still less harmful or tendencious rubbish. His faults have always been the result of a desire to make the theatre more lively, fuller of colour and movement, more theatrical.

Reinhardt, at Salzburg, is dictator ; and there are few dictators who, in an atmosphere as charged as that of Austria during the last few years, would have been content to maintain a purely *dramatic* festival, without allowing any political considerations to slip in.

In the past, too, he has always chosen his own path without caring for the advantages to be gained in another. The Deutsches Theater in Berlin was always a centre of opposition to the ex-Emperor's artistic ideals ; so that it was in the end regarded by him with suspicion—a pretext being that Reinhardt did not act himself in a command performance at Potsdam.

V

A peroration has a certain obituary tinge ; and to recall, even with the pleasure of recalling an artistic revolution, the beauty of dead theatrical productions is to recall the thinnest of ghosts. It is largely to Reinhardt, however, that we owe much prospect of pleasure in the stage of the immediate future, since his intelligent attitude to the theatre, liberated throughout the rest of Europe, has now reached England, if anonymously. And it is to him . . . and so on, and so on, and so on. All perorations are exactly the same.

LEON TROTSKY

By J. Hampden Jackson

Leon Trotsky

LEON TROTSKY

By J. Hampden Jackson

FEW men have more enemies than Trotsky. In the Soviet Union the Communist Party has banned his books and besmirched his memory. In the other nations of the world the governing bodies have refused him the right of asylum ; they think that " there is something wrong in the State of Denmark," which allowed him to deliver a lecture at Copenhagen in 1932. To them Trotsky appears to be spinning a monstrous Napoleonic Legend from his exile on the island of Prinkipo. It is true that no man since Napoleon has conducted campaigns simultaneously on so many fronts, and that, like Napoleon, Trotsky was under fifty at the time of his banishment ; but there the resemblance ends. To anti-Semites Trotsky is anathema—a Jew. To orthodox Jews he is an apostate, for he has had nothing to do with the faith of his fathers since he discovered that the old man who taught him to read the Hebrew Testament did not believe in God. And to Jew Nationalists he is a renegade :

> The national question, so important in the life of Russia [he wrote], had practically no significance for me. Even in my early youth, the national bias and national prejudices have only bewildered my sense of reason, in some cases stirring in me nothing but disdain and even a moral nausea. My Marxist education deepened this feeling and changed my attitude to that of an active internationalism.

Yet Leon Trotsky remains a Jew all through, from the cast of his countenance to the cast of his mind.

He was born in 1879, in the tiny mud-and-thatch farmhouse on the estate which his father David

Bronstein had just managed to buy. His parents worked every daylight hour and saved every kopeck. David Bronstein was a good farmer. When Leon at the age of seven was sent to the nearest Jew colony to learn his letters he realised that his father was an exceptional man. In Gromokley—it was typical of the Jewish agricultural colonies of South Russia, a tangle of tumble-down huts and filthy courtyards—the fields were tilled by German settlers ; the Jews stayed in the village, cobbling, tailoring, harness-making, and shop-keeping. They never rose above a state of primitive squalor. Even Abram Bronstein, the uncle with whom Leon lodged, was disreputable, though he was the most prominent man in the colony ; he ended by marrying a horse-thief's daughter. Leon was lonely in the colony, where he could make no friends among the children because he could not speak Yiddish (they spoke a Russian-Ukrainian dialect on the farm). When he came back home he was still lonely ; his book-learning seemed to have put a barrier between him and the farm life, and he spent his time writing a " magazine," making a collection of wicked words, filling an exercise book with speeches copied from a strolling player, and writing verses—

feeble lines which perhaps showed my early love of works but certainly forecast no poetical future.

Meanwhile, David Bronstein's affairs were prospering ; thanks to incessant work and relentless economies he was able to lease more land every year. He was proud of his son, who could read and write and keep the farm accounts—things he could never do till the end of his life. He decided to pay for a good education for Leon, and when the boy was nine he let Moissy Spentzer, a nephew with a literary bent, take him away to Odessa. Leon lived with the Spentzers :

Their apartment [he writes] was none too large. I was assigned a corner in the dining-room, behind a curtain. And it was here that I spent the first four years of my school life.

They were happy years. Leon went to a Lutheran school where, though he was not allowed to forget his racial origin, he was not baited for being a Jew. He worked prodigiously, had obvious talent, and was always first in his class. Yet he was not popular with the school authorities : they noted in him two unsympathetic characteristics, the first being a priggish hatred of injustice which led him to criticise the conduct of the staff, and the second a faculty for organisation which made him the guiding spirit in the successful barracking of an unpopular master. The characteristics which got him into trouble at school were to keep him in trouble for the rest of his life.

Leon's introduction to politics began when he was seventeen. He had been sent to Nicholeyev to finish his school career, and there had fallen under the spell of the revolutionary theories which were as much the normal intellectual food of the Russian undergraduate of the 'nineties as they are of the English undergraduate to-day. In Russia theory was apt to lead directly to practice, and the police, with the murder of Czar Alexander II fresh in their memory, could not be expected to look on revolutionary discussion with a tolerant eye. Rumours of Leon's activities reached David Bronstein, who made the long journey to Nicholeyev to offer his son the alternative between returning to the farm and going to Moscow to study engineering. In either case he must break with his revolutionary friends. There was a stormy scene : Leon refused ; and his father declined to continue his allowance.

Freed from the halter of a career, Leon plunged

into the business of educating himself. He went to
live in the cottage of a liberal-minded market gardener :

> Here six of us led a communal life. . . . We led a spartan
> existence, without bed-linen, and got along on stews which
> we made ourselves. We wore blue smocks, round straw
> hats, and black canes. In the town it was rumoured that we
> had joined a secret organisation. We read without method,
> we argued without restraint, we peered into the future
> passionately, and were happy in our own way.

It was all very adolescent, but none the less serious
for that. The tone of their talk can be imagined from
the political conversations in Dostoievsky's novels ;
but now, in 1896, the young men had got beyond
Nihilism. Leon's theory was that the solution to the
evils of the day lay in education ; he believed in those
days that tyranny and capitalism would fall like the
walls of Jericho before the blast of rational criticism
and inquiry. His chief opponent was the sister of
one of his friends, Alexandra Luovna Sokolovskaya,
a Marxist. She was ten years older than Leon and
laughed at the boy's romantic idealism ; revolution
would come, she said, only through the armed in-
surrection of the working class. Leon was not
convinced by Alexandra Luovna's presentation of the
Marxian case, but he was impressed by one aspect of
it, the necessity for getting in touch with the proletariat.
He managed to make contacts with working men in
Nicholeyev and Odessa—no easy task for a young
Jewish intellectual—and began to organise a party.
The success of his attempts at organisation was a great
surprise to him ; " The amazing effectiveness of our
work," he wrote, " fairly intoxicated us." It was a
still greater surprise to the police when they traced the
motive force of the South Russian Labour Union to
the little group they had long known as " the young
brats from the garden."

In 1898 Leon found himself in prison. First, there was an awful period of solitary confinement at Kherson, then nearly two years in the Odessa prison, where he found most of his friends from the garden. At some time during these prison years he realised that Alexandra Luovna was right : he became a Marxist. The realisation changed him from a romantic boy to a consecrated man. He was resigned when the trial came, and he was sentenced with his friends to four years' Siberian exile. On the way north, in the transfer prison at Moscow, Leon Davidovitch Bronstein and Alexandra Luovna Sokolovskaya were married by the rabbi-chaplain.

Nothing could have been better for Leon at this stage of his life than exile in Siberia. He lived at the Government's expense in a peasant-hut on the Lena, and had unlimited opportunity for work. With all the zest of a convert he set himself to read Marx. He emerged from the reading with a cubit added to his spiritual stature. In later life he was naïvely surprised at the failure of students to respond to Marx ; he could not understand the attitude of those who dismissed the Marxian plane of practical politics as ultimately insignificant, and he was shocked by the attitude of the professional Marxist,

who too often revealed himself as a Philistine who had learned certain parts of Marx's theory as one might study law, and had lived on the interest that *Das Kapital* yielded him.

For Leon, reading Marx was a vital experience ; not only did the dialectical method become his natural way of thought, not only did the materialist interpretation become the lens through which he habitually looked at the process of history, but behind the pages of Marx he had caught a glimpse of the fullness of life, a vision of a state of being in which mankind would be fulfilled. Like Saul on the road to Damascus, like Ignatius in the cave at Manresa, Leon Bronstein in Siberia had come to manhood.

The next step was to get into touch with the Marxist movement. He found a copy of *Iskra*, the paper which Lenin and others were editing from London and distributing surreptitiously in Russia. *Iskra* had an office in Samara ; Leon determined to join it. And so, leaving his wife and family—there were two baby daughters now, and escape was obviously impossible for them—he slipped away alone, writing in his blank passport the name of Trotsky, which had been the name of his warder at Odessa, and which was to cling to him for the rest of his life.

At Samara the *Iskra* people received him well—he had already made something of a reputation as a journalist by articles contributed to bourgeois reviews on life in Siberia and on the literary figures of the day ; they decided that he might be useful on the paper and sent him on to headquarters. Trotsky was highly excited ; he was going to meet the greatest living Marxists ! Early one autumn morning in 1902 he reached London and went straight to Lenin's lodgings. Lenin was in bed, but got up good-humouredly and spent the day listening to the young Jew's endless flow of talk. Lenin was ten years older than Trotsky ; he saw his faults—exuberance, over-confidence, audacity— and liked them : the youth was shockingly immature, but his heart was in the right place. Trotsky for his part was awed by Lenin and fascinated by Martov, another of the *Iskra* editors, a Jew, and a brilliant writer and talker. He did not know that Lenin was contemplating a breach with Martov and the *littéra-teurs* of the party. When the split came, when Lenin proposed at the Socialist Congress of 1903 that the party should commit itself to a policy of direct action and should admit only active revolutionaries, Trotsky voted on the side of Martov and the Mensheviks in opposition to the Majority or Bolshevik Party of Lenin.

It did not take Trotsky more than a few months to realise that Menshevism was futile, but he was not ready to accept the discipline of the Bolsheviks. He maintained an independent position between the two branches of the party, and was equally disliked by members of both, not only for his independence but for his fastidious taste in clothes and for his arrogant manner : somehow he always seemed to behave like a public figure instead of like a colleague.

The Russian Revolution of 1905 gave Trotsky his chance. To the surprise of the world the Russo-Japanese War turned into a rout of the Czarist armies and the collapse of the Czarist fleet. The breakdown was followed by sporadic risings of peasants all over Russia, by mutinies among the Baltic sailors, and by strikes in the industrial towns. The exiles hurried back to Petrograd, sick with anxiety lest the opportunity should pass before they could turn the situation to advantage. There was room now for a public figure among the Marxists. In Petrograd the workers set up a Council of Action, a *Soviet* ; when their first president was arrested, Trotsky was elected to the chair. For the fifty-two days of that first Soviet Trotsky lived in a whirl of action, with every faculty at full tension ; he needed all his powers of oratory to dominate the endless meetings, all his ability for organisation to hold the Executive Committee together. But no amount of personal energy could save the Revolution of 1905. In December the Petrograd Soviet was arrested, the Moscow strike broken. It afforded some bitter consolation to Trotsky in the midst of the ruin of his hopes to know that the part he had played was appreciated.

> His popularity [Lunacharsky says] among the St. Petersburg proletariat was very great by the time of his arrest, and was increased still further by his strikingly effective and heroic behaviour at the trial. I must say that Trotsky, of all the Social Democratic leaders of 1905-6, undoubtedly showed himself, in spite of his youth, the best prepared ; and he was the least stamped by the narrow *émigré* outlook which, as I said before, handicapped even Lenin. He realised better than the others what a State struggle is. He came out of the revolution, too, with the greatest gains in popularity ; neither Lenin nor Martov gained much. . . . But Trotsky from then on was in the first rank.

The first months of 1906 Trotsky spent in prison. Books and writing materials were sent in to him by Natalia Ivanovna Sedova, a Russian girl whom he had met working for the revolutionaries in Paris. (She has been his wife, in all except the legal sense, ever since.) He was elaborating the theory which he called—somewhat unfortunately for English ears— " Permanent Revolution," and which has since become known as Trotskyism, the theory which holds that modern industrial methods of production are not possible within national limits, and that, though the Socialist Revolution will come first in Russia, it must spread, if it is to survive, across national boundaries to establish first a European, then a world federation, of Socialist republics.

The prison period was ended by the condemnation of Trotsky to permanent exile at Obdorsk in the Arctic Circle. This would be very different from his first exile ; on the Lena he had been with his family, and the railway was near and mails frequent ; at Obdorsk he would be alone, the railway was fifteen hundred versts away, and one could not expect mails more than

once in two months in bad weather. The party that
left Petrograd consisted of fourteen prisoners and
fifty-five guards. The prospects of escape seemed
inconsiderable, but Trotsky had a faked passport in
the sole of one boot and gold pieces in the other.
When they reached Beresov, on the last stage of the
journey, he had a bad attack of " sciatica," and the
convoy had to march on without him ; they had no
fear of an attempt at escape at that time of year ; it was
February, the month of blizzards, and the town was
surrounded by a wilderness of snow for hundreds of
miles. Trotsky took his chance. He bribed a drunken
driver to smuggle him out of the town in a deer-sleigh.

> Early in the journey [writes Trotsky], the guide had a way
> of falling asleep frequently, and then the deer would stop.
> This promised trouble for both of us. In the end he did
> not even answer when I poked him. Then I took off his
> cap, his hair quickly froze, and he began to sober.

The drive across the snow desert lasted a week ;
then Trotsky made his way over the Urals on horse-
back, got safely on board a train on the Perm line, and
had the audacity to spend a short time in Petrograd
with Natalia Ivanovna and their son before he slipped
across the frontier to Finland, where Lenin and Martov
were hiding.

The period after 1905 was a sad time for Marxists.
In Russia there was no end in sight to the reaction
that had set in. In England, France, and Germany
more or less democratic politicians were lulling the
working class to a sense of security. The international
socialist movement was discredited, and was making
itself ridiculous by the squabbles among its leaders.
Among the exiles Lenin's group of Bolsheviks was
drawing farther and farther away from Martov and the
Mensheviks. To Trotsky it seemed that the only

policy in those hopeless years was to try to persuade Bolsheviks and Mensheviks to agree on a common platform, to abandon underground agitation, and to link themselves up with the Trade Union leaders of Europe. Lenin was bitterly opposed to this; he knew the fundamental insincerity of half the men who called themselves Socialists, and saw clearly that the only hope for Socialism was to keep that small nucleus of real revolutionaries, the Bolsheviks, free from compromise and official entanglement. Trotsky's policy was the cause of a long estrangement from Lenin throughout the years of his second exile.

They were not idle years for Trotsky. He toured the towns of Germany, lecturing; he founded a fortnightly paper, *Pravda*, which ran for three and a half years—an extraordinary life for an openly revolutionary periodical; he attended the party congresses at Stuttgart and Copenhagen. His headquarters were at Vienna, where Natalia Ivanovna joined him, and where a second son was born. They were poor enough, though Trotsky could always earn money when he could spare the time by writing for the *Kiev Missal*. As correspondent of his paper he went to the Balkans in 1912 and to Paris in 1914.

The outbreak of war ended whatever chances of success Trotsky's attempt to unite the Socialist groups might have had. The Trade Union leaders forgot their internationalism and turned into recruiting sergeants for Allies and for Central Powers. Trotsky kept his head and urged the workers of the world to boycott the war. It was a forlorn hope, preaching pacifism in 1914. Oddly enough, it led to a further estrangement from Lenin, who was horrified by the war but held that the working class must go through with it because inevitably it would turn into a civil war between the workers and the forces of Capitalism.

In Paris Trotsky managed to run a small Russian daily paper. He carried on peace-propaganda undisturbed until 1916, when the French Government, not unnaturally, expelled him. None of the fighting Powers would grant him a passport and he had to go to Spain and thence to the United States. In January 1917 he arrived in New York, and immediately got into touch with Russian exiles and plunged into the familiar life of underground propaganda. He was editing *Novy Mir* with Bucharin when the news of the March revolution and the fall of the Czar reached him.

It was intoxicating news. In a frenzy of excitement Trotsky rushed from office to office in New York getting his passports in order. At first everything went without a hitch, the papers were signed, and Trotsky and his family sailed from New York harbour. Then at Halifax the ship was stopped and searched by British naval authorities, who had orders to examine everyone bound for Europe. The excited little Jew was obviously suspicious ; he protested too much. The naval officers did not know anything about him, but they did not like his looks. They took him ashore and shut him in the camp for German prisoners at Amherst. Trotsky was beside himself. Day after day passed and no answer came to his cables. The prison authorities treated him as a criminal, even taking his finger-prints. A precious month was gone before the British Admiralty, in response to a request from Kerensky, sent orders that he should be allowed to resume his journey.

As soon as he reached Petrograd, in May, Trotsky saw that Kerensky had no understanding of the situation. It was absurd, Kerensky's attempt to make the proletariat who had deposed the Czar carry on the Czar's war with the Central Powers ; it was absurd, his attempt to rule the Russia of 1917 with a dual government of Liberal Ministers and Menshevik Soviets. Trotsky openly opposed Kerensky and was thrown into prison for two months. When he came out in September he was elected President (once again) of the Petersburg Soviet. He declared himself a Bolshevik : Lenin's uncompromising policy was justified now. He was the only leader who was not appalled by Lenin's pronouncement that *within a fortnight* the Bolsheviks must seize control of the Government, and he was the only leader who could realise the problems involved by that decision and who was capable of solving them.

> All the work of practical organisation of the insurrection was conducted under the leadership of the President of the Petersburg Soviet, Comrade Trotsky. It is possible to declare with certainty that the swift passing of the garrison to the side of the Soviet, the skilful direction of the work of the Military Revolutionary Committee, the party owes principally and first of all to Comrade Trotsky.

The words are Stalin's. In later years Stalin tried to swallow them :

> I have to say that Comrade Trotsky played no particular rôle in the October insurrection and could not do so, that, being president of the Petersburg Soviet, he merely fulfilled the will of the corresponding Party Authority, which guided his every step ;

but the earlier judgment has the truer ring.

Trotsky had sailed out of exile into history. For the next four years he was the most prominent figure in Russia, after Lenin. He had never thought of himself as a dictator :

> In spite of the experience of 1905, there was never an occasion when I connected my future with that of power. From my youth on . . . I had dreamed of being a writer.

He was an engineer who had mastered the dynamics of social forces ; that mastery made him a revolutionary thinker and an historian. Like so many men who have a talent for executive work, he had no taste for it, and when Lenin wanted to make him Commissar of Foreign Affairs after October he refused at first, making the excuse that as a Jew his appointment would be unpopular. But once he accepted power he gave himself full rein.

There was something superb about Trotsky in power. As representative of Soviet Russia at the Peace negotiations at Brest-Litovsk he hectored the diplomats of Imperial Germany and Austria-Hungary, and the newspapers of the world were filled for months with reports of his glowing advocacy of the case of Permanent Revolution. It was magnificent, but it was not war. " Neither war nor peace " was Trotsky's policy. It was with the greatest difficulty that Lenin brought him round to a sense of reality and persuaded him to sign the treaty in March 1918. Meanwhile, the Germans had been able to crush the Communists of Finland and to arm that State against the Soviet Union.

More exacting was the next task that fell to Trotsky. In 1918 the Bolsheviks were faced with enemies on six fronts—the English at Archangel, Yudenitch in Finland, the Japanese in the Far East, Kolchak and the Czechs in Siberia, Wrangel's army in the south, and the Poles in the west. Lenin had Trotsky appointed Commissar for War. Trotsky might protest with Cromwell, " I called not myself to this place," but there was no one else who could organise a New Model army in time to defeat the counter-revolutionary forces. A British agent, Bruce Lockhart, who had frequent interviews with him, asked himself fearfully in his diary, " Was Trotsky another Bar Cochba ? " Lockhart has described his appearance at this time :

He has a wonderfully quick mind and a rich, deep voice. With his broad chest, his huge forehead, surmounted by great masses of black, waving hair, his strong, fierce eyes and his heavy protruding lips, he is the very incarnation of the revolutionary of the bourgeois caricatures.

Sixteen Soviet Armies were soon familiar with this appearance : for the two and a half years of the Civil War Trotsky lived in a train, dashing ceaselessly from front to front, and the train became a symbol of victory for the Red soldiers, its arrival with supplies, news, and encouragement restoring the *morale* of the most isolated unit. Trotsky's methods were unorthodox and unprecedented (could anything be orthodox in that struggle when nothing was prepared and everything had to be improvised ?) ; his colleagues the Commissars criticised particularly what they considered his brutality in shooting Red soldiers suspected of disaffection. But Lenin was behind Trotsky ; he gave him a blank order-form at the foot of which was written :

> Comrades, knowing the harsh character of Comrade Trotsky's orders, I am convinced, so absolutely convinced of the rightness, expediency, and necessity, for the good of his cause, of the orders he has given, that I give them my full support.

Indeed, Trotsky was indispensable ; Lunacharsky, the Commissar for Education, wrote :

> Lenin is perfectly fitted for sitting in the President's Chair of the Soviet of People's Commissars, and guiding with genius the world revolution, but obviously he could not handle the titanic task which Trotsky took upon his shoulders, those lightning trips from place to place, those magnificent speeches, fanfares of instantaneous commands, that *rôle* of continual electrifier, now at one point and now another of the weakening army. There is not a man on earth who could replace Trotsky there.

On the relations between Lenin and Trotsky a whole

literature of controversy is being written. In English there is Ralph Fox insisting that " on every (fundamental) question, until Lenin's death, they proved to be in opposite camps," and Max Eastman stating with equal absence of qualification that " the friendship of Lenin and Trotsky ended as it began, with Trotsky in the rôle of Lenin's Big Stick." In every other European language Stalinites are writing to support the former view, Trotskyists to support the latter. The truth lies somewhere between them. Trotsky admired Lenin, but did not understand him. From 1903 until 1917 they were in opposition. From 1917 until Lenin's death in January 1923 they were in agreement and worked together ; there were differences of opinion —for instance, over the Brest-Litovsk treaty, and later when Lenin was in favour of a Bolshevik march on Warsaw and Trotsky opposed it—but for the most part they saw eye to eye. Especially during the last fourteen months of Lenin's life when he retired, paralysed, from direct control of the Government, Trotsky was his right-hand man. On four occasions during those last months, Trotsky forced the Central Committee of the party to accept Lenin's policy : first, on the question of foreign trade which Lenin insisted should, in a Socialist State, be under governmental control ; secondly, on the national question, when Stalin advocated the centralised repression of nationalities and Trotsky enforced Lenin's view that the nations in the Union should have full cultural autonomy ; thirdly, when Stalin suppressed an article which Lenin had written against the increasing oppressive bureaucratic character of the Government and Trotsky raised such a scandal that it was at last printed ; and finally, when on Trotsky's recommendation the Soviet Congress agreed to accept Lenin's policy of Economic Planning.

When Lenin died everyone outside party circles expected that Trotsky would succeed him. Lenin himself seems to have wished it ; in a document known as his Will he wrote : " The ablest of the Bolsheviks is Trotsky ; his defect is over-confidence. . . . Stalin is rude and disloyal." But Trotsky had little support among the other leaders of the party ; he had admired Lenin and had overridden the rest. After Lenin's death they let Stalin, the Secretary-General of the party, take control. No doubt they were right. Over-confidence is a serious fault, and it was time for a Thermidorian reaction in Russia, time to forget the dogma of Socialism for a while, so that the Soviet Union could build up its forces and make itself safe against boycott by the capitalist world. No doubt Trotsky would have provoked a capitalist coalition against Russia, with his slogan of Permanent Revolution.

So Trotsky was side-tracked. Throughout 1924 he was ill—some nervous disturbance which kept his temperature regularly above normal and baffled the doctors. In 1925 the War Ministry was taken from him and he was given work in the electrification and scientific departments. He plunged himself into the new branch with all his old vitality, but at the same time he kept up a running fire of criticism of the Government. Trotsky's suggestions were useful to Stalin—many of them Stalin adopted and put into practice as his own ; but it was dangerous to tolerate an Opposition within the Communist Party. In 1927 Trotsky was expelled from the party and sent to the Caucasus. In 1929 he was deported from Russia.

The Times [he reminds us] published reports that I had come to Constantinople by arrangement with Stalin, to prepare for a military conquest of the countries of the Near East.

For once *The Times* was misinformed : Trotsky had come to the Near East because no European country would admit him. At last he found a house on the island of Prinkipo, in the Black Sea.

The five years of Trotsky's third exile have been astonishingly fertile. The old stream of Socialist pamphlets have flowed unchecked from his pen, as clear and as buoyant as ever, penetrating to the bed-rock of contemporary politics. He warned us that the economic crisis of 1929 was no mere trade cycle, but the beginning of a world-wide catastrophe ; he predicted the bourgeois revolution which abolished the tyranny of Church and Monarchy in Spain ; he foretold the collapse which has overtaken the working-class movement in Germany. Analysing the provisions of the First Five-Year Plan he pointed to three weaknesses—the insufficient inducement to bring peasants voluntarily into collective farms, the inadequate provision for goods for immediate consumption, and the half-hearted attempt to solve the basic problem of railway transport ; these are precisely the three points on which the first plan is acknowledged to have failed and which the Second Five-Year Plan has been devised to remedy. Trotsky's political position now is essentially the same as it was in the time of his second exile : he stands for orthodox Marxism, and is the one man who is capable of uniting the international forces of Social Democracy and Communism.

But Trotsky has been more than a political journalist in these last years : he has established himself as an historian. All the unbounded Jewish *talent* in Trotsky, the imagination and vitality which made Bernard Shaw call him the Prince of Pamphleteers, backed by his deep understanding of the Marxian principle of history (which, however inadequate we may find it in a decade or so, is after all not unfitted to describe a Marxian revolution) ; all this, and the fact that he has felt under his hand most of the forces and shaped most of the events of which he is telling, makes him the ideal man to write the story of the revolution of 1917. *The History of the Russian Revolution* will become a classic ; it is no less comprehensive and no less balanced in style than that other history of a revolution written by an illustrious exile, Clarendon's *History of the Great Rebellion*. To potential readers who complain that history written by a protagonist must be biased Trotsky has an answer :

> The serious and critical reader will not want a treacherous impartiality, which offers him a cup of conciliation with a well-settled poison of reactionary hate at the bottom, but a scientific conscientiousness, which for its sympathies and antipathies—open and undisguised—seeks support in an honest study of the facts, a determination of their real connections, an exposure of the causal laws of their movement. That is the only possible historic objectivism, and moreover it is amply sufficient, for it is verified and attested, not by the good intentions of the historian, for which only he himself can vouch, but by the natural laws revealed by him of the historic process itself.

The world may have lost by Trotsky's banishment its greatest orator since Jaurès, but it has gained its greatest contemporary historian.

Trotsky will be remembered as a great public figure and a great historian, not as a great man. There is something inhuman about his intellectuality, his isolation. As an analyst he is unsurpassed, but he has never been an innovator ; in the four years of dictatorship he did not stand alone, he was an Aaron to Lenin's

Moses, and throughout the thirty-six years of his political life he has seen through the eyes of Marx. His vision is interpretative, not original ; it is the vision of a great executant musician, not that of a composer. His work has been to play Marx in the Concert of Europe ; and he may live to improvise yet another practical variation in the Marxian theme.

CHAIM WEIZMANN

By Lord Melchett

Chaim Weizmann

CHAIM WEIZMANN

By Lord Melchett

A DISTINGUISHED scholar, who has all his life been connected with the noblest elements of the English character and the English church, once wrote to me that if only Jesus of Nazareth had accepted the view that the Messiah was the deliverer who would always arise in the hour of Israel's need, and if Ezra had never carried through his rule about Jewish marriages, world history would have been very different during these last nineteen hundred years. This comment, which was made in the course of correspondence on Jewish affairs, embodies a great truth in regard to the development of the thought and morality of the Western World. It emphasises even more clearly the essential problem underlying the existence of Jewry, and I am prepared to accept my friend's comment, with the reservation that it was not so much a question of the view which Jesus of Nazareth took of the Messianic ideal as of the views held by St. Paul and the Apostles who ventured to interpret His teachings into the world at large, which mattered.

Speculation as to what the course of world history might have been had certain events not taken place or had things developed in another way has always been a fascinating exercise. Essays have been written on what would have happened if Napoleon had won the Battle of Waterloo, or if the conspiracy for the assassination of Julius Cæsar had failed, but there is perhaps no variation in history which would have so profoundly affected the development and the character of Jewry as that which my correspondent visualised. It must at once be realised that neither of the questions which he raises would in any way have involved the ethical or moral teachings of Christianity or of Judaism. These would have remained unimpaired, but the authority with which they were told to the world would have been very different.

Had these broadened liberal views, which might now achieve a large measure of acceptance among educated people, been adopted nineteen hundred years ago, they would have made no difference to the dispersion of the Jewish people under the Roman Empire. They would, nevertheless, have been driven forth and scattered into the different countries of Europe. But their history from then on might have been very different. While they would still have been confronted with the difficulty of being strangers in every land, they would have avoided violent persecution due to religious differences, and had the marriage ban not been imposed, they would have been rapidly absorbed into the nation among which they dwelt.

As a matter of historical fact, for centuries they have suffered persecution due to differences both of race and religion, and have, as a result, become a people different from all others. They have remained a people without a land, surviving under conditions which should, by all the laws of nature, have spelt an early elimination, and which have forced upon them characteristics far different from those which are recorded in the Bible, simply in order that they should survive.

It is a curious commentary on all this to read in the current press that a community of Jews in the Mainz district of Germany, consisting of three hundred families, has, during the recent German elections, abandoned its homes and taken to the woods and the fields, in order to save the lives of its members. In the pleas that they have put forward to the Government and to other communities, they have said that they did not care what became of their houses and their property, or under what conditions they might be absorbed into other communities, provided they could save their lives alone. To a large extent, this has always been the condition of Jewry, which has for centuries been driven to preservation of life itself, as against all other interests. This violent contact with reality, coupled with the amazing subtlety of mind which enforced intellectual recreation naturally produces, has created that strange being, the modern Jew, who, up to a short time ago, existed almost exclusively in Poland and Russia.

The Jewish communities of England, Germany, France, Holland, and elsewhere were smaller in number and lived among more enlightened people. On the whole they enjoyed such a different fate that it is hard to compare the two. Therefore it was from the Jewry of Eastern Europe that the perpetual cry for emancipation arose, and emancipation of an entirely different character from that which was desired in the West : not an emancipation of civic rights alone, in the countries in which they undertook and carried out the obligations of citizenship, but for a higher emancipation ; a country of their own where they could once more be a people with their own culture and develop their own national and racial attributes, without incurring the hostility of other nations. This desire to be themselves, for their own sake, instead of trying to become either Poles or Russians or Germans or Dutchmen, had, for many years, expressed itself in what was termed the Zionist Movement, before the Austrian journalist, Theodor Herzl, aroused by the injustice of the Dreyfus case, commenced a campaign, as the result of which he hoped to re-acquire Palestine for the Jewish people.

At that time the country lay a desert and derelict

under the dead hand of Turkish administration, and while Herzl succeeded in interesting many of the rulers of Europe in his project and succeeded in gathering around him those Jews of Eastern Europe who had, years before, debated and discussed this conception, the Turkish Government remained entirely unmoved.

Amongst those who were prominent in this movement was Chaim Weizmann from Russia. From early boyhood the question of the destiny and fate of his people had troubled him, and at the early age of twelve he had written a letter to his teacher in which he said that he conceived it to be the case that it was principally England among the nations of the world which was destined to help in the redemption of Israel.

As a young man he went abroad to study chemistry, both in Germany and in Switzerland, and took an exceptionally brilliant degree in Freiburg in 1898, at the age of twenty-four. There he was easily drawn into the circle of Zionist adherents who centred round Herzl. It was at Geneva that he met his wife, herself a student of medicine, later practising as a doctor, who, sharing all his enthusiasms, has herself played a leading part in the Zionist Movement, from then up to the present time. To Weizmann Zionism was something more than a pure question of physical emancipation. The continued existence of Jewry as a people, in spite of such appalling difficulties, seemed to him to show that there was an inner purpose and an inner meaning in Jewry. The redemption of Israel, as a practical concept, could only be achieved in Palestine, that strange and mystical country with which the greatness of the Jewish people has been associated throughout human history.

In 1901 Weizmann was already the leader of a party of young men within the Zionist Movement, who called themselves the Democratic Zionist Party. Associated with him were Martin Buber, Berthold Feiwel, Leo Motzkin, and others, and their desire was for an immediate and practical expression of their ideal in the foundation of schools, colonies, and even a University in Palestine itself. Their programme was to commence the work, on however small a scale, to emerge into an era of practical effort, and to leave behind the period of discussion and political manœuvring which had up to that date been the only manifestation of Zionism. Herzl and his associates had a different view. Their inclination was to take no positive action of their own, but to collect a vast fund with the ultimate idea of purchasing Palestine *en bloc* from the Turks, hoping to achieve this objective as a result of combined efforts, of the power of money, and of political pressure brought to bear by those nations of the world who sympathised with their cause.

Weizmann's admiration of England and English ways soon afterwards brought him to Manchester, where he came in 1903 as a lecturer in chemistry at the University, and England has remained his home ever since. It was an important year for him in many respects. It was in that year that he put forward to the Zionist Congress a detailed study of the proposal to found a Jewish University in Palestine. It was in the same year that the British Government, represented by Joseph Chamberlain, moved by the eloquence of Herzl and the justice of his cause, suggested to him that as apparently he could not persuade the Turks to enter into any arrangement in regard to Palestine, he should take over Uganda from the British Government and use that as the new centre for the foundation of a home for Israel.

Herzl was, by this time, deeply disappointed by his failure to achieve an objective which had, at the outset, seemed eminently practicable. He felt behind him a great movement whose hopes he had aroused and felt it was necessary for him to produce practical results. There were many attractions in the Uganda scheme, which can be seriously discussed even to this day, and Herzl had the support of such eminent individuals as Zangwill and Greenberg when he seriously suggested to the Zionist Congress that they should accept Chamberlain's proposal. This idea, however, cut completely across the whole of Weizmann's conception of the destiny and the existence of his people. He was the leader of the storm of protest which followed Herzl's suggestion and which not only defeated it but overwhelmed it. It is all the more remarkable to consider that this rejection of a large and fertile tract of country in a not unfavourable climate and under the protection of the mighty British Government, was made at a time when Eastern Jewry had, but a few months before, been overwhelmed by a series of the most terrible pogroms.

In order to understand the force that lies behind the Zionist Movement, it is necessary to realise how at that time the choice was made between purely physical emancipation and an emancipation that had a spiritual significance which it is hard to put into words, but which lies in the mystical association that no difference of politics, nor time, nor humanity itself can alter, between the Jewish people and the land of Palestine. The Uganda policy was defeated, and for the time being it appeared that nothing existed to take its place.

The most important work that was being done in Palestine was being achieved by Baron Edmond de Rothschild, who was, at his own expense, founding and developing colonies on a small scale in that country, but at the Congress in 1907 Weizmann's policy was successful to the extent that the Zionist Organisation opened a Palestine office in Geneva and founded a Palestine Land Development Company. From then on until 1914 Zionist activity continued in a small but thoroughly practical way, building up colonies, opening schools, developing villages, and the foundations of the great city of Tel-Aviv, which to-day contains some 70,000 souls, were laid by some ten or a dozen men with a few thousand francs at their disposal. In addition to his Zionist activities, Weizmann was deeply engaged in chemical researches, and during this period acquired a reputation which placed him among the leading chemists of England, a fact which was to play a dominant part in the future history not only of himself but of his people.

When war broke out in 1914 Weizmann, who had long since adopted British citizenship, was already a leading figure amongst the research chemists who were called upon to assist in the developments which the abnormal conditions of the Great War rendered vital. He had, during the intervening years, through his Zionist work, come into contact with Arthur Balfour, and while he had made a considerable impression upon him, as Herzl had made upon Chamberlain, he did not altogether succeed in convincing him that the Zionist ideal was anything more than a romantic dream, which, while arousing philosophical speculation of a most interesting character, was altogether outside the realm of practical statesmanship. All the same, a personal contact had been established on the basis of a mutual friendship and esteem, which added another vitally important stone to the foundations which Weizmann was laying, and upon which the structure of practical Zionism was to be erected.

In 1915 Weizmann's supreme opportunity occurred. It was the culmination of the great efforts that he had made during the course of a life of unsparing work and intellectual activity. As a scientist and statesman he had developed, not only his personal reputation, but his powers of achievement to a point which enabled him to seize upon an act of fate and the conjunction of events for the benefit of his people. In the abnegation of personal advancement, he achieved at one blow a result which decades of effort and vast expenditure might have failed to bring about.

Working for the Admiralty, Weizmann perfected his most subtle and complex method of obtaining alcohol from wood, at a time when this material, absolutely vital for the production of explosives, was becoming impossible to obtain in sufficient quantities owing to the submarine campaign and the abnormal conditions of war.

Mr. Lloyd George has himself described the occasion and said that, confronted with one of the most serious crises with which he was ever beset in the Ministry of Munitions, we were saved by the brilliant scientific genius of Dr. Weizmann. Both he and all the Allies felt a deep debt of gratitude, and when they talked to him and asked, " What can we do for you in the way of any honour ? " he replied, " All that I care for is opportunity to do something for my people." So it was that at that critical moment when the Zionist cause was under its darkest cloud and the Jewish people was divided across the face of Europe by the rage of war that the true greatness and imagination of a statesman brought their policy to fruition.

Within a comparatively short space of time, developments of the campaign in Palestine and the desire of the Allied Powers to ensure the interest of the Jewish people throughout the world, produced additional practical reasons to support the Zionist cause. In 1917, as the result of prolonged delicate and arduous negotiations, the Balfour Declaration was made by the British Government, and accepted by the Allied Nations. It laid down, in effect, that the British Government, supported by the other Governments in question, viewed with favour the establishment of a National Home in Palestine for the Jewish people, and would co-operate to bring this about.

In March of 1918 Weizmann, who was now recognised throughout the world as the leader of the Zionist Movement, went to Palestine to act as liaison officer between Great Britain and Palestinian Jewry, and on July 21, he laid the foundation-stone of the now flourishing University of Jerusalem, the establishment of which he had urged upon the Zionist Congress fifteen years before.

The next two years were periods of intense activity. From the Balfour Declaration to the establishment of the Mandate under the League of Nations, was a long and difficult path. It was Weizmann who did the work requiring endless patience, infinite tact, and incredible persistence. In 1921 he was elected President of the Zionist Organisation, a place which he occupied continuously until 1929. Throughout he displayed the same qualities of constructive statesmanship which had distinguished him from the beginning. He gathered around him outstanding figures of Jewry on both sides of the Atlantic, notably Louis Marshall, Felix Warburg, and the first Lord Melchett, and together they worked to establish a wider basis for the Zionist Movement in the creation of the Jewish Agency, which should include those many indefinable but powerful forces of world-Jewry which were not identified with the Zionist Organisation. The Jewish Agency finally emerged in practical form at the Congress of 1929 in Zürich, and almost immediately commenced that series of disasters which had such a marked effect upon the career of Weizmann and the progress of the Zionist Movement.

By 1929 a large measure of prosperity had been created in Palestine. Great areas of land had been reclaimed and colonised. New towns, new villages, new industries, new schools had grown up. The Zionist Movement had begun to acquire a definite technique in the acquisition of land and the settlement of immigrants, and what had been in 1919 a wild experiment, could be viewed by its creators with satisfaction in 1929 as a highly successful and rapidly developing movement. As the result of their efforts, over 100,000 Jews had been successfully settled in Palestine, and while relations with the Arab population had for a long time been strained, and while the difficulties of the British Government had been multiplied by the increasing complexity of a new civilisation growing with unprecedented rapidity, there was no reason to expect any serious check to the growth of the movement.

It must, of course, be realised that, in spite of the fact that this development far outstripped anything that any British Colony or Dominion had proportionately achieved during the same period, and that while outside difficulties and obstacles were of an entirely exceptional character, the absorption of 100,000 Jews into Palestine in ten years seemed a very small thing to the 3 million Jews in Poland, the 800,000 in Rumania, the 500,000 in Czechoslovakia, and the other great aggregations, amounting in all to some 8 millions, that still remain in touch with the Zionist Movement outside the borders of Soviet Russia, where something like a third of the total Jewish population seemed to have been hopelessly swallowed up.

So it came about that when the disturbances of 1929 broke out and the Arab population fell upon the un-

armed Jews, creating a situation which was really more
serious in its political than in its physical aspect, and
which resulted in a temporary abrogation by the
British Government, represented in this case by Lord
Passfield, of its sympathetic attitude, the outcry in the
Jewish world was directed ˄t once against those
leaders who had been responsible for the direction of
Zionist policy for the previous decade.

There is no occasion here to enter into the vagaries
and difficulties which beset the position at this time;
the Inquiries and Commissions that followed and
eventually the reassertion of the Mandatory principle
by the Prime Minister (Mr. Ramsay MacDonald), in a
letter to Dr. Weizmann in 1930. It is sufficient to
point out that during that time the brilliant progress of
the Zionist Movement received an inevitable if temporary check which gave the opportunity for the
" Opposition " parties, which always exist in every
movement, to deploy their forces to the fullest extent.
At the same time, two of Weizmann's staunchest and
ablest supporters, Louis Marshall and the first Lord
Melchett, both died, leaving him more isolated than
ever. When the Zionist Congress met again in 1931
Palestine was still in a condition of depression. According to the Opposition everything that had happened
was Weizmann's fault. Had he been stronger, more
tactful, more energetic, and had longer vision, all the
difficulties could have been avoided ! According to
them the Arabs could have been placated, the British
Government (distraught with many other problems
far more vital to the British Empire) persuaded, not
only to give apparently the whole of its time and
attention to Palestinian affairs, but also to have appointed
none but its most able and brilliant administrators
to look after this small country about the size of Wales !

The difficulty, in fact, was the impossibility of

bringing within a reasonable comprehension of each
other a large number of highly intelligent men of
different views, each having grown up in a different
country, each approaching life with a slightly different
historical background, each viewing world affairs from
a different angle. In addition, the vast majority of
Zionists being Continental, therefore possessed an
extremely imperfect knowledge of English psychology
and English conditions. The difficulty of welding
them into a whole when things are going well is serious
enough, but the power of holding them together in
these exceptionally difficult and almost inexplicable
circumstances was more than Weizmann, wearied by
his Herculean efforts, was able to exercise. Both he
and the first Lord Melchett had officially resigned their
respective positions of Chairman of the Jewish Agency
and President of the Zionist Organisation on the day
the White Paper was published. At the Congress in
1931 he confirmed his resignation in his inaugural
address, and did not put himself forward for election
as President. Among other matters which had
contributed to the confusion of Zionist affairs was
the economic crisis which commenced in 1929 and
seemed to have culminated in 1932. This economic
blizzard which swept across America and Europe
not only deprived the Zionist Organisation of some
two-thirds of its normally available funds, but
also created an economic pressure in Central and
Eastern Europe, which made the demand for Palestine
development and for opportunities for immigration
even more insistent than ever before. Weizmann's
task of holding up the Zionist edifice, shattered by such
gigantic forces, was completely hopeless.

But the history of events since then has shown the
amazing resilience and power which exist with Zionism.
Many a man who had experienced what Weizmann had

been through would have considered himself justified in abandoning all his Zionist work, and turning once more to his scientific studies. He might justly have argued that he had done all and more than could be expected of any single man for his people. After such treatment as he had received he might feel that they could look after themselves. But here the greatness of the individual showed itself in the fact that far from adopting such a course, he at once placed himself at the disposal of the Movement in any way in which he could be of use to it, and proceeded upon a long and arduous tour through South Africa, as the result of which, in a most critical period of Zionist finance, the amazing sum of £200,000 was raised and retrieved the economic situation.

Meanwhile, those same world forces which seemed inevitably about to destroy Zionism, suddenly appeared as most favourable factors, working as a stimulus to increased activity. To the Jews of the middle class throughout Europe and America who still had a few thousand pounds available and whom it had in the past been impossible to interest in the work in Palestine, it seemed that their fortunes and the work of their lifetimes were to be swept away in the universal depression. Jews who know their own history are sufficiently well aware that in cases of severe economic depression anti-Semitism invariably arises in its most virulent form. Signs of the latter were not lacking, and the two forces together exerted a pressure which resulted in a tremendous flow of capital and individuals to Palestine, who found opportunities awaiting them there, based upon the work that had been so successfully carried out in the previous decade.

By 1932 Palestine had become the isolated and outstanding example of a country prospering in a world of ruin. It was, I think, in the year 1932 almost the only country with published figures which succeeded in balancing its Budget and achieving a surplus, and certainly the only country which published statistics on labour questions showing a practical absence of unemployment.

In 1933, when the Hitler menace struck Jewry the greatest blow it has received since the Middle Ages, world Jewry turned to Palestine as a practical and real factor in a situation of unprecedented difficulty. Jews who had avoided Zionism like the Plague became supporters of the movement both in opinion and in act. Weizmann had the extraordinary experience of addressing a meeting at Woburn House on a platform where his two immediate supporters on either hand were Mr. L. G. Montefiore and Mr. Anthony de Rothschild, who had been signatories to a letter protesting against the Balfour Declaration as being impracticable and undesirable sixteen years previously.

In the turmoil of events which followed from March 1933, Weizmann stood out as the greatest leader in Jewry. It is true that he was not elected President by the Zionist Congress held in Prague in August, but the internal politics of that occasion are far too recent to be recorded here. It is sufficient to assert that the assassination of Mr. Arlosoroff in Palestine, at that time head of the Zionist Executive in that country, inextricably complicated the already difficult position.

It is almost impossible to produce an adequate biographical sketch of a man while he is not only still alive but at the height of his powers. It is only possible to achieve any sort of perspective if one assumes that the subject of the biography has ceased to be. Had it been Weizmann and not Arlosoroff who was assassinated in Palestine at the beginning of this year the estimate that would have been made of him by his contemporaries would have placed him head and shoulders above all other Jewish leaders of the period as a great man of his people, and of all time, and would have placed him in this position, not only for his achievements, but for the ideals which had guided him.

No statesman and no politician has been free from criticism either during his lifetime or after his death upon the smaller points of policy and upon the methods which he has adopted. In the history of England the Pitts, Gladstone, Disraeli, Canning, and Palmerston have been torn to pieces for their political methods, while at the same time they have been idolised as the great statesmen of their country. In practical achievement Weizmann stands quite alone. What Herzl dreamed, he did ; what others talked of, he carried into practical effect ; while others quarrelled and disrupted, he unified and consolidated.

To have started from the obscurities of a Russian village and to have arrived as a liberator, if not of a people, at any rate of its most cherished ideal, is an achievement which has rarely been paralleled in the annals of history. The ideal that the Jew shall call at least one country his own, and that his by tradition, by affection, and by the historical association of thousands of years ; the ideal that there he should exist, not on sufferance, but as a right, with equal manhood, equal opportunities, equal conditions in which to develop a normal human existence, has become a living fact in the National Home in Palestine.

But it is not only in the realm of practical achievement that Weizmann will stand out. As a dreamer of great dreams, as an idealist, he will always hold his place. In the face of all physical difficulties he, as an eminently practical statesman, continued to believe in the mystical and apparently hopeless conception of the destiny of his people. He continued to believe throughout the disillusionment that comes with the difficulties of actual working, that Jewry has a mission, that Israel can be redeemed, and that once more in some strange way which none of us can even dimly foresee, the world will be enriched by a great message which will and can only emerge from Palestine when Israel dwells once more with it

Presented in this way, nis achievement becomes absorbed in and identified with the personality and achievement of Israel itself, in its great effort—an effort which can perhaps be most easily understood by a remark my late father made, standing one evening upon the ruins of Babylon, when he turned and said : " You see, had it not been the case centuries ago, that some small proportion of our people were prepared to return to Palestine, to be the Zionists of that day, we should all have perished in the civilisations that perished with Babylon. It is only because of those few who returned at that time, that you and I are able to stand here and look upon these ruins. And where are those that took us into captivity in Babylon ? "